"In *Caring for Creation*, Mitch Hescox ... ... compelling evidence, grapple with in ... ..., and propose crucial solutions regarding one of the most urgent crises of our day. As people of faith, we can lead a global conversation toward action—action that will save millions of lives and bear witness to a creative and loving God who cares about all people."

—**Stephan Bauman**, president, World Relief

"Evangelicals defend our belief that God created the world, yet we sometimes fail to conserve it. *Caring for Creation* presents a compelling case for a clean energy revolution that will protect future generations from the ravages of climate change. A must-read for any Christian seeking to be consistently pro-life."

—**Galen Carey**, vice president of government relations, National Association of Evangelicals

"This is a fabulous read! Engaging, informative (sometimes shocking), practical, and deeply spiritual, this book will equip us for action."

—**Dr. Joel C. Hunter**, senior pastor, Northland, A Church Distributed

"It was characteristic of biblical prophets that they sounded clear warnings about the realities of the present and impending consequences. But they also called for radical practical change and never lost the anchor of hope in God. This book is prophetic for our generation in all three ways: realism, practicality, and biblical hope."

—**Rev. Dr. Chris Wright**, author, *The Mission of God*; international ministries director, Langham Partnership

"The cross is much more powerful than any of us can imagine. There God reconciled to himself all things, restoring us and creation itself to a right relationship with him. Mitch Hescox and Paul Douglas write of this marvelous purchase and the amazing role God has given us to tend the bit of Eden that's left. I know from wonderful times spent with both of them that their words reflect their hearts and their life's work. The calling they describe here is a calling worth fulfillment."

—**Bob Inglis**, former U.S. Representative, South Carolina; director, Energy and Enterprise Initiative

Caring
For
Creation

Caring For Creation

The Evangelical's Guide to Climate Change
and a Healthy Environment

MITCH HESCOX
AND PAUL DOUGLAS

BETHANYHOUSE
a division of Baker Publishing Group
Minneapolis, Minnesota

© 2016 by Mitch Hescox and Paul Douglas

Published by Bethany House Publishers
11400 Hampshire Avenue South
Bloomington, Minnesota 55438
www.bethanyhouse.com

Bethany House Publishers is a division of
Baker Publishing Group, Grand Rapids, Michigan

Printed in the United States of America

Library of Congress Control Number: 2016938459

ISBN 978-0-7642-1865-1

Scripture quotations are from the Holy Bible, New International Version®. NIV®. Copyright © 1973, 1978, 1984, 2011 by Biblica, Inc.™ Used by permission of Zondervan. All rights reserved worldwide. www.zondervan.com

Cover design by Dan Pitts
Cover photo by Alexander Haase / Getty Images

Authors are represented by Red Sofa Literary

16 17 18 19 20 21 22   7 6 5 4 3 2 1

In keeping with biblical principles of creation stewardship, Baker Publishing Group advocates the responsible use of our natural resources. As a member of the Green Press Initiative, our company uses recycled paper when possible. The text paper of this book is composed in part of post-consumer waste.

To a loving Savior, who created a beautiful blue world for us to tend. To my grandchildren, Shea, Morgan, Orion, Jackson, Ben, and those yet to be born—may you inherit a creation not filled with extreme weather, rising sea levels, or dangerous temperature rises. To my beautiful wife, Clare, who endures her driven workaholic husband, and finally, to my parents, John and Betty, who taught me a faith in Jesus and the value of hard work.

—M. H.

To my amazing sons, Walt and Brett, and generations to come.

—P. D.

Contents

Introduction

An Unlikely Cause

The trouble with weather forecasting is that it's right too often for us to ignore it—and wrong too often for us to rely on it.

Patrick Young

Guide me in your truth and teach me, for you are God my Savior, and my hope is in you all day long.

Psalm 25:5

"Paul, what's going on with the weather?" As a TV meteorologist, I get that question a lot these days. As time goes by it gets harder to answer.

How is the weather where you live? Is it what you remember growing up? No? It's not your imagination. Our weather is a hot mess. It's almost as if Mother Nature picked up a remote control, put the seasons on fast-forward, and dialed extreme weather up to a 10.

In the late 1990s and early 2000s it was increasingly freakish weather—not Al Gore—that tipped me off that something had changed. Patterns were shifting. Something was off.

I didn't set out to talk about climate change. It wasn't on my radar. I was just doing my job, tracking daily weather, attempting to connect the dots and make sense of the atmosphere. Like many TV meteorologists, I had been traumatized by weather at a tender age. Tropical Storm Agnes flooded my home in Lancaster, Pennsylvania, in June of 1972. It put the fear of God into me—and made me want to study severe storms. I graduated with a meteorology degree from Penn State, where I provided weekend weather for a TV station in Wilkes-Barre/Scranton, Pennsylvania. The station set up a backyard weather set, appropriately called The Backyard. The news director took me out back, pointed, and said, "Paul, if you're standing outside, at least you'll get the current weather right." Great vote of confidence. I went on to work TV meteorology jobs in Connecticut, Chicago, and the Twin Cities, which is where my wife and I raised two amazing boys and I launched a series of weather technology companies on the side. I've always had an entrepreneurial itch, an urge to tinker and invent.

One of my earliest companies, EarthWatch, brought 3-D weather graphics to TV stations in the early nineties. Steven Spielberg used our special effects for *Jurassic Park* and *Twister*. I actually have a line in *Twister*, pointing to Doppler radar as a monster F-5 tornado is just starting to spin up. "Hey, Bryce, you better come here and take a look at this!" If you sneeze or blink, you'll miss my big scene. My last residual check from Warner Brothers? One cent. So much for my film career.

Another business, Digital Cyclone, put Doppler radar on cell phones in 2001—it was one of the first companies to put an app on a mobile device. I sold that business to Garmin in 2007 to focus on personalizing the weather. Since 2010, AerisWeather has built TV studios, hired meteorologists, and launched two national weather channels. Today we personalize weather for businesses and consumers, leveraging new technologies that bring the story down to an audience of one. We brief Fortune 500 companies on global weather risks and threats, helping weather-sensitive companies operate more efficiently, profitably, and safely with desktop and mobile applications. I have risked my money for things I believe in. I've sweated out payroll. I've failed, regrouped, and reinvented. I am an entrepreneur—and I believe the power of markets can help transform our world for the better.

For the record, I was raised Baptist, Presbyterian, and Lutheran. My parents were always shopping for a better deal. I'm a Christian, serial entrepreneur, meteorologist, Eagle Scout, and staunch Republican. My youngest son graduated from the Naval Academy and flies helicopters in the Pacific, so we're a military family too. And I acknowledge that colorless, odorless carbon pollution—the waste gas of progress—is spiking the storms I'm tracking on my maps, representing a legitimate risk, one we should pay close attention to. All of which—together—makes me the rough equivalent of an albino unicorn. Pray for me.

"Speak the truth, even if your voice shakes," my father taught me. My dad fled communist East Germany and found success in America. A loyal Reagan Republican, he taught me to see the world as it is, not as we wish it to be. The only thing I inherited was a sense of curiosity, a strong work ethic, and a belief that citizenship comes with rights *and* responsibilities—a belief that actions have consequences and nobody has a right to threaten the common good or twist the truth for perpetual profit. We should be open to facts, even when they make us squirm.

Being open to data, facts, and science doesn't make you liberal. It makes you literate. Scientifically literate. It means you favor data, facts, and evidence over conspiracy theories, manufactured misinformation, and cherry-picked industry spin. We live in God's creation and — as stewards — have a holy obligation to treat it as the remarkable gift it is.

Like Paul, I (Mitch) also grew up in Pennsylvania. In my case, it was in a tiny western Pennsylvania town that before my birth was home to the largest firebrick manufacturing plant in the world. For those who don't know, firebricks are the masonry that line blast and other high-temperature industrial furnaces. In the early 1960s, people there still dreamed of the once-thriving facility that had employed thousands but now sat rotting away. What jobs remained came from coal mining. My dad was a coal miner, as were my grandfathers and many uncles, cousins, and other relatives.

Coal was in my blood. My early playgrounds were un-reclaimed strip mines a hundred yards from my back door, chasing down tadpoles in water fouled with sulfuric streaks of bright red and orange. One vivid memory growing up was the volunteer fire department's siren going off in the middle of the day. In our town, that siren typically wasn't a warning of a fire but rather a coal mine accident. On more than one occasion, those accidents involved at least one of my family members.

My dad used to take me to the small coal mine that my paternal grandfather owned in the late 1930s and 1940s. Even in the mid-1960s, the vestigial traces of the abandoned mine remained. Dad would point out the four-foot-high mine entrance and explain how after high school he worked on his hands and knees mining a twelve-inch seam of coal. The lesson learned was a powerful message in hard work that remains with me today. It is part of the Protestant work ethic that defines who I am.

It is no wonder that I spent the first fourteen years of my professional life in the coal industry. After college, I began a career selling, installing, and eventually designing equipment for use in coal processing or in coal-fired utilities. My last coal-related position saw me designing grinding equipment for pulverized coal boilers in China, India, and South Africa.

Coal is part of my legacy, but so is God. Growing up, a little white country church was the center of life. My family attended everything from church suppers to vacation Bible school. We frequented gospel music events at my church or one of the other small churches that dotted the villages throughout central Pennsylvania. In that faith community, I dressed up on Christmas Eve in the stereotypical bathrobe and sang "We Three Kings," arose early on Easter morning to hear my Aunt Marie sing at sunrise service, and preached my first sermon in the fourth grade. However, like so many young people then and today, my late teenage years saw me questioning God. Particularly troubling were questions about creationism versus evolution. These questions challenged my faith and led me to run away from God and head west to pursue a degree in geology. I would later call this my Jonah experience.

Even as I questioned God, he never gave up on me. My life forever changed on a Thanksgiving weekend camping trip during my first semester at the University of Arizona. While visiting the Sonoran Desert, more than two thousand miles away from family, I encountered the truth, relevance, and mystery of the Bible.

> For since the creation of the world God's invisible qualities—his eternal power and divine nature—have been clearly seen, being understood from what has been made, so that people are without excuse.
>
> Romans 1:20

When we returned to our campsite after a grueling day of hiking, Jesus found me. In the midst of my wilderness, I chanced upon a giant saguaro cactus framed by the setting sun, deep red and arching across the entire horizon. In my mind's eye, the saguaro became Jesus's cross and the bloodred sun became God's son; I fell on my knees and gave my life back to Jesus. That moment sparked my journey back to God and my eventual exit from the coal industry to start my second career and first calling—pastoring a local church for eighteen years—before several nudges from God got my attention again. I knew he was leading me to a national ministry, but with gifts and graces centered on evangelism, telling the good news of Jesus' love, and caring for the least of these, a Christian relief and development organization seemed the right fit. Little did I realize that my primary gifts would lead me to heading the Evangelical Environmental Network, the largest evangelical group dedicated to caring for creation. Our tag line is "Creation care is a matter of life."

Caring for people, overcoming challenges, and providing a tangible hope for the future with clean air, pure water, a solid economy, and good jobs—that's what we and countless others are attempting to do.

For Mitch and I, our interest in stewarding the earth was no overnight epiphany. Our conviction built gradually; a slow-motion realization that the threat was real and people of faith have a moral obligation to step up.

Today we humans are changing the chemical composition of the atmosphere. We are fiddling with the planet's natural thermostat—poking at the climate system with a long, sharp, carbon-tipped stick, and then acting surprised every time the weather bites back. And the weather is biting back with increasing frequency and ferocity. We are the volcano, conducting an experiment that's never been done before—on a planetary scale, on the only home we have: God's home.

In a day and age of scammers, hackers, hucksters, special interests, and media hype, you should be skeptical about *everything*. Skepticism is a healthy defense mechanism. Some of the most skeptical people alive are scientists. In fact, science is organized skepticism. Science isn't a quest for ultimate truth, but a process of correcting your errors.

There's a place for science and a simultaneous faith in real absolutes, like a sovereign, all-powerful God. We believe in God. Science, we test. And careful observations in the real world confirm that our actions are having unintended and profound consequences.

In this book we'll certainly tackle the top issues and questions. Is global warming real? Is climate change really spiking storms and changing weather patterns? Is this something we have to worry about for our kids and grandkids? Are we truly threatening God's creation, or is this all an elaborate hoax—a plot to grow big government, increase regulation, and take away our individual freedoms? Is there a pragmatic, commonsense, *conservative* response to climate change—one that doesn't grow government but empowers the markets to create the clean energy alternatives, services, and products we're going to need to not only survive but thrive no matter what nature hurls at us?

The goal is to turn down the volume of rhetoric, antagonism, and name-calling and focus on finding common ground: faith-based solutions that elevate personal responsibility and conservative values to tackle problems that face us.

"We just don't have the winters we used to have." That's what Mitch's ninety-year-old dad said recently at his kitchen table. "Snow used to stay around all winter, and we had a lot more of it. I think it's time to do something about this climate change stuff before it's too late."

The former coal miner gets it, and many of us feel it inside. Actions have consequences, and we are all accountable. We are caretakers of God's creation. The Bible includes nearly a thousand references to creation care and stewardship. Conservatism isn't à la carte. It can and should apply to the very thing that sustains us.

Mitch and I agree, acting on climate change is not about polar bears—it's about our kids. It's not about political agendas—it's about being a disciple of Jesus Christ. It's not about killing jobs—it's about making everything we do stormproof, resilient, and sustainable. That's the purpose and hope contained in these chapters.

The situation isn't hopeless and we aren't helpless.

CHAPTER 1

An Accumulation of "Coincidences"

Warming of the climate system now is unequivocal, according to many different kinds of evidence. Observations show increases in globally averaged air and ocean temperatures, as well as widespread melting of snow and ice and rising globally averaged sea level. . . . Climate is always changing. However, many of the observed changes noted above are beyond what can be explained by the natural variability of the climate.

American Meteorological Society (2012)

A man should look for what is, and not what he thinks should be.

Albert Einstein

Whatever happened to normal weather? Earth has always experienced epic storms, droughts, and floods, but lately it seems the treadmill of daily disasters has been set to fast-forward. God's grandiose symphony of the seasons—the magical, predictable ebb and flow of the atmosphere—is playing horribly out of tune, sounding like a fourth-grade orchestra, with shrill horns, violins screeching off-key, and cymbal crashes coming in at the wrong time. Something has changed.

It wasn't a slick documentary that got this meteorologist off the dime. It wasn't even dire warnings from climate experts. It was the increasingly inexplicable weather showing up on my daily weather maps in the late 1990s and early 2000s.

Imagine your favorite college football team running out onto the field, but all the players have the flu. They suited up, but they're slow, groggy, and sluggish, running the wrong routes, more prone to confusion and injury. Our weather has the flu. It isn't apparent every day, but many days I shake my head and think, *Haven't seen that before.* A cosmic coincidence? A symptom of more people living in vulnerable locations? Or a liberal-leaning, hype-happy media publicizing extremes that have always been there since the creation?

Doctors rely on science. They look at symptoms. And based on observations, evidence, and best practices built up over many centuries, they make their diagnosis and suggest specific treatments. Drug companies may push a specific medication, but your doctor is supposed to be objective and unbiased, looking out for your best interests. So it is with the scientists telling us that earth is heating up.

Some people ask, "What's a few degrees, Paul? Who cares?" Fair enough. But remember the last time *you* were a few degrees warmer? Chances are you felt miserable. There were visible symptoms: cold sweats, a rash, nausea, sneezing, and sniffling.

The atmosphere and oceans are running a low-grade fever, and the symptoms are showing up in the weather: rashes of record heat, drought and wildfires, sneezes of violent winds from a parade of severe storms, sniffles of rain falling with much greater intensity, often resulting in biblical flooding. A warming climate

CHICAGO—A surge in the incidence of flooding as a result of more extreme precipitation events across the Chicago area in recent decades has been among the most noteworthy developments on the climate front here. A study by Dr. Dave Changnon, climatology professor at Northern Illinois University, found warm season dew points have been increasing at Midway Airport since the 1970s. This is likely playing a role in the increased incidence of warm season rainfall. There may be other effects from our warming climate here as well. The latest EF-4 twisters and one of eight earliest EF-4 tornadoes touched down in northern Illinois within two years of one another. Area farmers will tell you that planting has, as a general proposition, started earlier as growing seasons and the period of frost-free readings has increased.

Counterintuitively, the growing frequency of arctic latitude warm pools and blocking has locked the Midwest into a northwest steering flow aloft in recent winters—a flow pattern that has lasted into the summer and produced subpar summer temperatures. The irony is that warming in the arctic seems to be driving cooler than normal temperatures into the nation's midsection, while producing searing heat from the Plains and Western U.S. northward, into the Canadian tundra and even interior Alaska.

Tom Skilling, Chief Meteorologist, WGN-TV

isn't sparking new storms, but it is spiking existing storms and increasing the potential for jaw-dropping, headline-grabbing weather extremes.

When in doubt, meteorologists rely on their Amish Dopplers. You know what an Amish Doppler is, right? *A window*. We are all hardwired to look out the window and react to the weather floating above our house, but don't mistake that for climate. Don't look at your thermometer for evidence of warming; do look at your yard for tangible signs of a slow-motion warming trend: a longer growing season, new plants and flowers growing that weren't there forty years ago, more poison ivy and allergens, and new pests and invasive species that your parents didn't have to worry about. Patterns are shifting. Across much of the United States spring arrives ten to fourteen days earlier than it did just twenty years ago.[1] The evidence is there, but it's slow and subtle—until a megastorm comes along and clubs you over the head. And the weather-clubbing appears to be happening with greater regularity.

A warmer atmosphere holds more water vapor, increasing the potential for summer floods and extreme winter snows, especially along the East Coast. Wet areas are getting wetter—dry areas are trending drier. You've heard the expression "weather on steroids"? We're turbocharging the storms that would have formed anyway—loading the dice in favor of more extreme weather events. "All storms are 5 to 10 percent stronger in terms of heavy rainfall," explains Dr. Kevin Trenberth at the National Center for Atmospheric Research in Boulder, Colorado. Even a couple-degree rise in temperature increases the potential for convulsions of wild weather that threaten life and property. "It means what was a very rare event is now not quite so rare," Trenberth adds. How many times do we have to be smacked over the head before we sit up and pay attention?

DENVER—Extreme drought, destructive wildfires, tornado warnings at night in Denver, the devastating floods of September 2013, a new record for the number of days over 90 and 100 degrees—are these random events in Colorado or are they related to global warming? They are probably linked to a warming climate. With a gradual warming of the planet, our regional climate is likely to become drier on average over the next one hundred years. The result will be more wildfires, lower water levels in our reservoirs, and more frequent droughts.

Mike Nelson, Chief Meteorologist, KMGH-TV

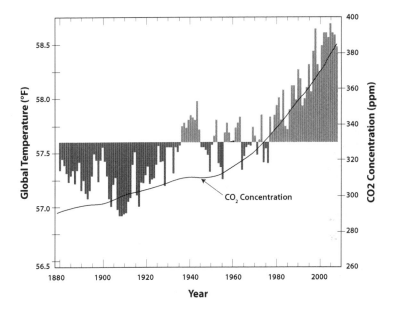

To this day people confuse weather and climate. Climate is what you expect, weather is what you get. Weather is, *Do I need shorts or a jacket?* Climate is the *ratio* of shorts to jackets in your closet. It's a little like comparing CNN to The History Channel. Weather is chaotic, random, and hard to predict—short-term gyrations in a much bigger climate system that responds to inputs: solar radiation, subtle changes in earth's orbit, volcanoes, and greenhouse gases, which are essential to trapping warmth and making life possible.

But we've been fiddling with earth's thermostat. Every day, by burning fossil fuels, we pump 87 million tons of carbon pollution into the atmosphere. That equates to approximately 32 billion metric tons of carbon dioxide (CO2) released into the sky every year, worldwide.[2] The average American emits about fifteen tons of CO2 into the air every year just by driving a vehicle.[3] This invisible, heat-trapping blanket of man-made chemicals is the rough equivalent of four Hiroshima-sized atomic bombs' worth of extra heat *every second*. Put another way, that's 400,000 atomic bomb blasts of additional heat energy *every day*. According to the U.S. Department of Energy, well over one trillion tons of greenhouse gases have been released in the last fifty years. That's one trillion hot-air balloons' worth of CO_2 and methane. *We are the volcano*. Earth just passed 400 parts per million (ppm) of carbon in the atmosphere in 2015, the highest level in the human record. These heat-trapping gases are building up at a historically unprecedented pace.

We are changing the chemical composition of the atmosphere and the oceans. Why care? Since the dawn of time there's been a tight correlation between the level of greenhouse gases and global temperatures. When carbon and methane levels shoot up, so does the temperature. This is based on ice core samples drilled out of Greenland and Antarctica, not climate models.

The atmosphere has never experienced such a rapid buildup of CO_2 and other heat-trapping chemicals in such a short period. For the first time, this warming blanket of man-made greenhouse gases is warming both hemispheres—and there's no obvious astronomical trigger.

It's good to be skeptical. Every time it snows, professional cynics question whether the climate is really changing. *"How can the*

RALEIGH/DURHAM—The most obvious threat to North Carolina relates to sea level rise and our fragile Outer Banks. Many houses on the barrier islands that face the ocean used to be on the third row before rising waters and erosion washed rows 1 and 2 away. And it's not just hurricanes and tropical storms that cause the problems. Any storm that possesses a large enough wind field, with much of it having an onshore component, can cause enormous damage. With sea levels continuing to rise, one can only wonder what the future will hold for our tourism industry, which depends so heavily on vacationers frequenting our beaches.

Greg Fishel, Chief Meteorologist, WRAL-TV

atmosphere be warming if I'm cold, Paul?" There's a word for this: Winter. If it ever gets to the point where it doesn't snow anymore, when Canada runs out of cold fronts, our planet will have much bigger problems. Let's hope it doesn't come to that.

Billion-dollar weather disasters are on the rise worldwide, fueled by an increasingly volatile climate.[4] Major disaster declarations in the U.S. are steadily increasing due to hurricanes, snowstorms, droughts, and severe thunderstorms. (An eye-opening chart of climate-related disasters and related costs can be found at http://www.ncdc.noaa.gov/billions/time-series.) From 1990 to 1999, there was an average of six emergency declarations issued each year, and from 2000 to 2009, there was an average of fifteen issued every year.[5] Insurance companies report that weather-related losses have tripled since the 1980s, from an average of $10 billion to nearly $50 billion every year.[6] Fourteen of the fifteen warmest years on record, worldwide, have occurred since 2000, according to NASA and NOAA (the National Oceanic and Atmospheric Administration). The odds of that being a random fluke are 650 million to 1, according to statisticians.[7]

The twentieth century was the warmest in one thousand years. The first decade of the twenty-first century was the warmest decade ever observed. And 2015 was the warmest year on record across the planet, followed by 2014. And 2016 should set a new global record for warmest year ever observed. Globally, the ten warmest years in the past 134 have all occurred since 2000, except for 1998, according to data from NASA.[8] The first fifteen years of this century were among the top-twenty warmest years on record. Experts say the odds of that are 1.5 quadrillion to 1 (a quadrillion is a million billion).[9]

I'm all for coincidences and serendipity, but at some point you connect the dots, scratch your head, and acknowledge it may be a trend, not a fluke.

Connecting the dots—tying extreme events to a rapidly changing climate—is known as *attribution*. Research is ongoing, but there

DETROIT—As the planet warms, more ocean water is evaporating into the atmosphere, and this increased atmospheric humidity is what storm systems use to generate precipitation. But it's not just rain. Here in southeast Michigan, we are also seeing it in the form of . . . snow! Yes, a warmer world has translated into more snow for the metropolitan Detroit area. It shocks people when I tell them that five of our top ten all-time snowiest winters have occurred since 2004, and a sixth occurred in the early 1980s! Remember Boston's record snow in the winter of 2014-2015? That was Detroit the previous winter. Precipitation records in Detroit date back to 1874, which is long enough to show a changing climate's impact.

Paul Gross, Meteorologist, WDIV-TV

is little doubt a warmer, wetter atmosphere is already flavoring the weather. I'm just scratching the surface, but here are some of the trends that got our attention.

1. Heat Waves, Droughts, and Wildfires

The link between climate change and extreme heat is firmly established. Due to global warming, rare and extreme heat events impact a percentage of the globe ten times greater than they did from 1951 to 1980.[10] In the past several years, the global area hit by extremely unusual hot summertime temperatures has increased fiftyfold.[11] Over the contiguous United States, new record-high temperatures over the past decade have consistently outnumbered new record lows by a ratio of two to one.[12] There is a high probability that the 2011 heat wave in Texas and Oklahoma and the devastating heat wave that gripped Russia in 2010 were made worse by a warming climate.[13] A recent study in the journal *Nature Climate Change* found that the 1.5 degrees Fahrenheit of global warming since the start of the Industrial Revolution had quadrupled the probability of moderate heat extremes.[14]

Put simply, if the earth really is warming we should see more record highs than record lows. Which is, in fact, what we're observing. The warming in the mid-latitudes of the northern hemisphere is increasing at a rate roughly equivalent to walking south thirty feet every day. This rate is about a hundred times faster than most climate change observed in geological records, according to Stanford University climate scientist Ken Caldeira.[15]

Droughts are also becoming more prevalent, lasting longer, and impacting more people. Warming triggered by human emissions is thought to have intensified the grueling 2011 to 2014 California drought by 15 to 20 percent; by some estimates the worst dry spell in twelve hundred years.[16] The number of large wildfires in the U.S. has nearly doubled since the 1980s, and the average length of wildfire season has grown by more than two months.[17] Over the past twelve years, every state in the western U.S. has experienced an increase in the average number of large wildfires per year compared to the annual average from 1980 to 2000. Higher temperatures, increased evaporation, surging populations, and changes in fire suppression practices are all factors fueling an increase in fire, most pronounced over the western United States.

2. More Intense Precipitation Events

Paul's home state of Minnesota has experienced five distinct 1-in-1,000-year floods since 2004.[18] Eight of the ten wettest years for daily precipitation in the upper Midwest have happened since 1978.[19] Nationwide, the U.S. has experienced at least six separate 1-in-1,000-year flood events since 2010.[20] Coincidence? Perhaps, but the rain seems to be falling harder than it did for your parents or grandparents.[21] Recent years have brought historic flooding to Pensacola, Nashville, Detroit, Atlanta, Tampa, Boulder, and a vast stretch of South Carolina, Texas, and Louisiana. Observations confirm that heavy precipitation events are on the rise. New England

Contiguous U.S. Extremes in 1-Day Precipitation

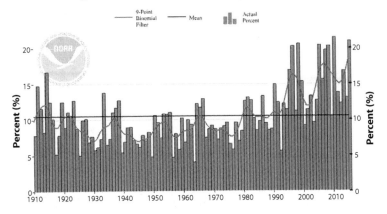

and much of the Northeast has experienced a 71 percent increase in heavy precipitation since 1958.[22]

Why is this happening? A warmer atmosphere holds more moisture. There's nothing controversial about that statement. It's basic physics. Every 2-degree Fahrenheit of warming means roughly 8 percent more water vapor floating overhead; more fuel to "juice" storms and squeeze out heavier summer rains and winter snows.

The biggest increase in damage from weather events over the past decade came from severe storms, which NOAA classifies as tornadoes, hailstorms, severe thunderstorms, derechos (storms with strong straight-line winds), and flash floods. There were forty such events with losses exceeding $1 billion from 2004 to 2013, compared with thirteen between 1994 and 2003.[23] Blizzards are getting supersized too. Data shows extreme regional snowstorms were twice as common from 1961 to 2010 than 1900 to 1960.[24]

Some, but not all, of the uptick in natural disasters can be explained by population growth and more people living in harm's way, including building in risky flood zones. Still, flooding caused the majority of global disasters between 1994 and 2013, accounting for 43 percent of all recorded events and affecting nearly 2.5 billion people.[25]

3. Sea Level Rise

The water is rising, which makes sense since warming water expands. New research suggests seas are rising at the fastest rate in the last twenty-eight centuries.[26] The water can't expand downward, so water levels have to rise; tangible symptoms of a warming ocean. In Miami, it now floods on a sunny day with a full moon—no storms required. Melting ice from Greenland and Antarctica is further accelerating sea level rise. If anything, climate models have been conservative. A 40 percent decrease in polar ice was measured from September 1980 to September 2015.[27] This ice doesn't add to sea level rise, but it's a good barometer of the warming underway.

The eight-inch average sea level rise that has already occurred worldwide since 1880 makes the impact of hurricane storm surge flooding worse.[28] Even generic Nor'easters pack more of a coastal flooding punch than they did just a generation ago. A twelve- to fifteen-inch sea level rise in New York Harbor since the 1700s enabled Hurricane Sandy to reach an additional 80,000 homes in 2012.[29] The insurer Lloyd's of London estimated that higher sea levels increased Sandy-related losses by 30 percent, with an additional $8 billion in damage in New York City alone.

Coastal flooding is on the rise. Water damage has surged over the past ten years, in large part caused by increased hurricane activity.[30] NOAA reported twenty-three flood and hurricane events with losses exceeding $1 billion between 2004 and 2013, compared with sixteen from 1994 to 2003. According to NASA, sea level rise is happening faster than originally predicted; an additional three-foot rise may be, in their words, "unavoidable."[31]

Nearly 150 million people around the world live within three feet of sea level, threatened with dislocation and subsequent civil unrest. For them, climate change and rising seas will be more than

MIAMI—Most of our planet's 7 billion people now live in cities. Historically these have been built near lakes, rivers, and
oceans—sources for food, water, and transportation. For the
hundreds of millions living in coastal cities, the end of this
century and beyond looks to bring significant existential challenges. This includes those residing in the South Florida mega-
lopolis that extends from Miami to Palm Beach. From my office
window in Miami I can see a fraction of the trillions of dollars
invested in a super-infrastructure designed to make our city
life more comfortable. But I can also see a menacing Atlantic
Ocean, which already frequently inundates our streets with
salt water, even on sunny days.

That's one big reason why climate change is such a big
concern. We can't move entire cities like New York or Shanghai
because sea level rise will soon be inundating them. Miami,
specifically, is the top-ranked city in the world in terms of as-
sets at risk. It's a city that's indefensible against higher sea level

just a minor inconvenience. It may evolve into the civil rights challenge of the twenty-first century, because the first to be impacted
are the world's poor, those least able to adapt to rising seas and
weather-on-steroids. Not only is melting ice from Greenland and
Antarctica accelerating sea level rise, but more than 3.5 trillion tons
of water have melted off of Alaska's glaciers since 1959, when Alaska
first became a state. That's enough to fill more than one billion
Olympic-sized pools.[32] As many as 90 percent of the world's glaciers
may be lost in the next few centuries if heat-trapping greenhouse
gases continue to rise at current rates.[33]

4. More Intense Hurricanes

Although impacted by myriad factors, including El Niño–
triggered wind shear, dry air, and Saharan dust, hurricanes get their
fuel from warm ocean water. The warmer the water, the greater the

because it sits on top of porous limestone. No dike can be built to stop seawater from penetrating far inland, contaminating drinking water supplies, and lifting the water table to the point of inundation along a very flat and low landscape. As I write this, there are dozens of new buildings in various phases of development along Miami's coast. No one seems to be concerned about the long-term viability of these edifications, nor the infrastructure that supports living in them. Insurance rates are still low relative to the risk (greatly subsidized by the government). This won't go on forever, probably not even into the late twenty-first century. Eventually, hundreds of thousands of people who thought their families could remain comfortably anchored in their Magic City homes will have to consider a Plan B, especially for their children and grandchildren, due to sea level rise caused by global warming.

John Morales, Chief Meteorologist, NBC 6

potential for strengthening. The Pacific basin has seen a string of devastating Category-5 hurricanes in recent years, which may be, in part, attributed to warmer water. Typhoon Haiyan, which decimated the Philippines in November 2013, came ashore with sustained winds of 197 mph, roughly equivalent to a twenty-mile-wide EF-5 tornado. Studies suggest a possibility of fewer storms in the future, but the storms that do spin up may be more intense.[34] Although quiet in the Atlantic, 2015 was a record year for hurricanes and typhoons in the world's largest body of water, the Pacific Ocean.[35]

5. Ocean Acidification

Trees and oceans absorb CO_2, but there's a natural limit to how much these "carbon sinks" can soak up. The world's oceans currently absorb about a third of human-created CO_2 emissions, close to 9 billion tons every year. Surface water in the world's oceans is 30 percent more acidic than it was two hundred years ago.[36] The

31

impact on sea life is still unclear, but more acidic oceans threaten coral reefs, biodiversity, and the food chain we all depend on.

6. More "Weather Whiplash"

The arctic region is warming twice as fast as the United States and other mid-latitudes, impacting north-south temperature gradients and, subsequently, the jet stream—the high-speed river of air in the upper atmosphere. Preliminary research suggests a 12 percent drop in jet stream winds, creating a wavier pattern, one in which weather systems slow, sometimes becoming stuck.[37] When weather stalls, bad things can result: extended floods—and on the flip side, more prolonged and intense heat waves and droughts.

All over we are seeing wilder swings in temperature and moisture. Dry areas are, in fact, getting drier and wet areas are trending even wetter. An almost surreal blocking pattern combined with a nearly stationary firehose of tropical moisture from Hurricane Joaquin to dump up to twenty-six inches of rain on South Carolina over three days in October 2015. That's a year's worth of precipitation for most northern cities. New research from the University of Minnesota suggests a rapidly changing climate may be sparking fewer summer storms over the Northern Hemisphere.[38] There are more days between rain events, but when it does rain, it comes down in a tropical deluge. The CEI, or Climate Extreme Index from NOAA's National Climatic Data Center, shows a 30 percent increase in regions of the United States experiencing either extreme drought or extreme flood since 1910. (Another attention-getting chart is found at https://www.ncdc.noaa.gov/extremes/cei/graph.) I'm no rocket scientist, but I detect a steady upward trend since the 1970s, and the trends are becoming more obvious each year.

We are witnessing multiple fingerprints of a rapidly changing climate. The weather has become even more erratic, manic, and

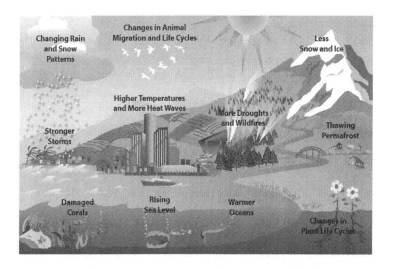

unpredictable: patterns shifting, storms and droughts stalling for longer periods of time, extreme rainfall events on the rise, all while seas warm and ocean levels rise. At some point, denying climate change becomes a little like denying there's a war when artillery shells are landing next to your house.

Acknowledging a changing climate doesn't rest on a slender thread of evidence. From shrinking summer ice at the top of the world impacting the jet stream, to an uptick in weather extremes, shrinking glaciers, more acidic oceans, a spike in debilitating heat waves, devastating droughts, and summer downpours, our climate is already changing. Like a doctor examining a feverish patient, we are witnessing symptoms of a warmer, more volatile climate system.

So now what? All this feels too big, too depressing, too overwhelming. Most of us are trying to get through the week, pay our bills, and keep the wheels on the bus. *Don't give me one more thing to worry about!* Psychologists tell us that we avoid or deny a problem when there is no obvious, straightforward way out. But there are solutions. There is a path forward. One thing remains constant: *We are stewards of God's creation.* We all have a vested interest in treating God's gift with care, respect, and reverence. In this book, Mitch and I will share ideas and solutions both big and small for improving our world, helping our families and those around us.

We all have a set number of sunrises and sunsets remaining. We're here to glorify our heavenly Father and care for his kingdom, to be good stewards of what we've been given, to care for those we know and those we don't know. That isn't optional. Jesus made that abundantly clear.

> He will reply, "Truly I tell you, whatever you did not do for one of the least of these, you did not do for me."
>
> Matthew 25:45

We'll figure this out. Mitch and I are optimists. Climate change is more than an environmental problem or an economic challenge. It's a moral and spiritual imperative. A new level of climate volatility and weather disruption will affect everyone, but the poorest among us will be hit first, and hard. Pay close attention and keep an open mind. The signs are already showing up—directly above your head.

It's not your grandfather's weather anymore.

CHAPTER 2

It's Not About Polar Bears

Modern man has been upsetting the balance of nature and the problem is drastic and urgent. It is not just a matter of aesthetics, nor is the problem only future; the quality of life has already diminished for many modern men.

Francis Schaeffer

People certainly like talking about the weather, but in today's polarized society, most folks aren't willing to talk to people with different worldviews or understandings of faith. It's far too easy to ridicule or even dehumanize another person because they believe differently. It's as if one group has all the answers and there's no reason to value the thoughts of another. What makes this even more concerning for the evangelical Christian is Jesus' command "Love each other as I have loved you."[1] From the political right, I (Mitch) have been attacked with death threats, told I'm going to hell, called a liar, and maligned in all sorts of news articles and blog posts by brothers and sisters in Christ.

One group produced a resource titled "Resisting the Green Dragon" shortly before I became president of the Evangelical Environmental Network. The gist of the resource is to link people like me to the dragon of the book of Revelation, portraying those who care for God's creation and especially climate change as evil. In an attempt to lighten and brush off the silliness of this attack, I often wear a green suit when talking with local churches. Standing six-foot-three and weighing 250 pounds, I mention being called the Green Dragon but much prefer to be known as the Jolly Green Giant. I invite the congregation to be the judge.

The left isn't much better. Often, I have been asked to speak to liberal groups on reaching conservatives, to help them to become aware and take action on climate change and creation care

Why should we be concerned about the environment? It isn't just because of the dangers we face from pollution, climate change, or other environmental problems—although these are serious. For Christians, the issue is much deeper: We know that God created the world, and it belongs to Him, not us. Because of this, we are only stewards or trustees of God's creation, and we aren't to abuse or neglect it. The Bible says, "The earth is the Lord's, and everything in it, the world, and all who live in it" (Psalm 24:1).

When we fail to see the world as God's creation, we will end up abusing it. Selfishness and greed take over, and we end up not caring about the environment or the problems we're creating for future generations. It's not surprising that some of the world's worst environmental damage was done by the old atheistic regimes of Eastern Europe.

I hope you won't lose your concern for these issues, for they are important. But don't lose sight of something that is even more important: your relationship with God. Is Christ first in your life, and are you seeking to follow Him every day?[2]

Billy Graham (2008)

in general. As I walk up to the podium, I ask, "How many of you would self-identify as evangelical Christians?" Never does a hand go up. I then ask, "How many of you would consider yourself pro-life?" At that point usually eyes start to glare (and if the stares were knives, I'd be long gone), and I get the reaction *Who does this guy think he's talking to?*

Liberals love the polar bear. For the past decade, the polar bear has become the iconic image of climate change. Movies have been made depicting the polar bears' current struggle as the ice pack diminishes and survival becomes more difficult. We might feel sorry for the polar bears, recognize them as part of God's creation. But if we are honest with ourselves, polar bears won't drive us to action. A good friend, Rachel Gutter, heads up the U.S. Green Building Council's Green Apple Schools initiative. It's the leading movement to protect our children from indoor air pollution, toxic chemicals, and other factors that impact our children's health in the location that most kids spend a large portion of their lives: the classroom. She is much more colorful when addressing the same issue. Rachel, a petite young woman, stands as if an *Ursus maritimus* (the scientific name for a polar bear) herself and says, "It's not about our [bleeping] polar bears; it's about our children." Understanding the need to defend our kids' health, provide pure air and water, and provide for a good economic future challenges the integral struggle that may tip the seesaw for climate action.

We live our lives as a seesaw, trying to balance work, family, values, and faith. Most of us act only when our everyday life balance and values are impacted in such a way as to upset that tipping point; only when an issue touches the center of our being—who we are and those we care about—are we willing to listen, learn, and take action. When issues like climate change arise, it's very easy for us to dismiss or deny them because they put one additional stress into

**American Academy of Pediatrics
Letter to EPA**

Eating foods containing methylmercury can expose the brains of adults, children, and developing fetuses to harm. Critical periods are during pregnancy and in the early months after children are born. Mercury exposure can lead to developmental birth defects and interfere with neurological development. Pregnant women who consume fish and shellfish can transmit that methylmercury to their developing fetuses, and infants can ingest methylmercury in breast milk. Children can also become exposed by eating contaminated fish.[5]

our everyday lives. That's why being pro-life helped me to understand that creation care is truly a matter of life for our kids, the majority of the world's poor, and even many of the economically disadvantaged in the United States whose homes border some of the most toxic air, foul water, and polluted land.

Pro-life for me is caring for all of life. As Focus on the Family put it recently, pro-life is not a political statement, it's a way of life.[3] In a recent National Association of Evangelicals (NAE) statement on end-of-life, the NAE states we are pro-life from womb to the tomb.[4] That expresses my own theology as well as many evangelical Christians'. We are concerned about life from conception until natural death. The unborn child is very important to us, but so is each child of God at every stage of life.

A few years ago, I testified before the United States House of Representatives Energy and Power subcommittee on mercury emissions from coal-fired power plants and the threats posed to our unborn children's brains as a pro-life matter. Congressman John Shimkus (a Republican from Illinois) proceeded to lecture me with Scripture after Scripture. After several minutes of soliloquy, I attempted to interrupt the Congressman and asked to answer his questions. His reply: "I'm doing good enough by myself, thank you." He went on to say, "The 'life' in 'pro-life' denotes not the quality of life, but life itself."[6]

If we believe Jesus' words in John 10:10 ("I have come that they may have life, and have it to the full,"[7] or as other translations phrase it, "abundant life," or "of life abundantly"), how can we not be concerned with the quality of life? I pray for my kids and grandchildren to have a quality of life. I have dreams of good health, following the career God is calling them to, and finding the wonderful fruit of life given by the Holy Spirit. That's pro-life being more than a political statement. Without doubt, pro-life should be about not ending a pregnancy, but also assuring the right for the opportunity to abundant life. We must have a whole or entire life theology that cares for the unborn and born child alike.

As pro-life evangelicals, we want children to be born healthy, unhindered by the ravages of pollution even before they take their first breath. The medical community has long known the environmental impacts on our unborn children. The once-assumed chemical protection a mother gives her developing child is untrue. One of the body's protective shields against brain damage, called "the blood-brain barrier," is not fully developed until after the first three years of life. Thus, in the unborn child, toxins can cross this incomplete barrier and accumulate in the brain, causing developmental disabilities and brain damage, resulting in lowered intelligence and learning problems. One study found "the resulting loss of intelligence causes diminished economic productivity that persists over the entire lifetime of these children."[8] In economic terms, the poisoning of our unborn children's brains costs between 60 and 106 billion dollars in the United States per year.[9]

As just one example, recent studies have shown that smog and volatile organic compounds (VOCs) including hydrocarbons, benzene, formaldehyde, and air toxins have a disproportionate impact upon life in the womb. University of Pittsburgh researchers found evidence of low birthweight babies associated with proximity to unconventional natural gas wells in Butler County, Pennsylvania,[10] and in a Colorado study, birth defects in a rural area were linked to methane production.[11]

Unfortunately, many in our pews have not yet accepted the connection. Until our communities understand and identify the problems using our values, our communities have no way to internalize and act on problems our children face. Often when speaking before a congregation, I start my presentations asking, "Will you please stand if you have a child or grandchild with asthma? Autism? ADHD? Allergies? Cancer?"

By the time I get through asking those questions, it's not uncommon for up to 90 percent of the congregation to be on their feet. I look around the room to see the number of lives and families that are impacted. Then I simply state, "If you're not concerned about caring for God's creation, you should be, because our failure to be good stewards touches every one of our family's lives. Creation care is a matter of life."

According to the American Lung Association, more than 35 million kids in the United States live in areas with unhealthy air.[12] The latest childhood epidemics with strong links to petrochemicals and fossil fuel energy—asthma, autism, ADHD, and allergies—impact as many as one in three children in the U.S.[13, 14] Dr. Philippe Grandjean states, "We are facing massive prevalence of brain dysfunction, autism, and many other signs of ill health due to development insults. Because the exposures to toxic chemicals happen worldwide, the adverse effects are appearing now as a silent pandemic."[15]

It's very clear that what we put into God's creation returns to us in very alarming ways. Back in the 1960s a woman had a one-in-twenty chance to develop breast cancer in her lifetime; now the frequency is one in eight. This rapid increase in cancer rates led my friend, Dr. Matthew Sleeth, to study the Bible, convert to Christianity, and then leave his career as an emergency room physician and start a ministry, Blessed Earth, teaching creation care and becoming a bestselling author.

Unfortunately, the breast cancer news isn't good. According to Dr. Philip Rosenberg of the National Cancer Institute, breast cancer rates are expected to increase by 30 percent by 2030.[16] That means the number of women diagnosed with breast cancer will jump to 441,000 in 2030 from 283,000 in 2011. The one glimmer of light in the research shows a lower mortality rate.

While the modern medical field understands a great deal about breast cancer, much is still unknown. Doctors know that breast cancer rates are higher in the developed world than the majority world. They also know that only 30 percent of women with breast cancer have known risk factors such as genetics, late menopause, or having children later in life. The cause of 70 percent of breast cancer diagnoses is, of yet, unclear. Nevertheless, a growing body of research points to the environment; especially suspect are chemicals and plastics that act like hormones in the human body. A large body of plastics such as bisphenol-A (BPA), high density polyethylene

Pesticide Risks

Chemicals are part of God's creation. When used responsibly they contribute to our quality of life. But we must insist on robust standards to protect our children and families from the harmful effects of dangerous chemical combinations. The lives of one Pennsylvania family were changed in the summer of 2005 when a neighbor misused Organo Phosphate Pesticide, Dimethoate 4EC. The family's dogs and children were playing nearby when the pesticide was sprayed. "Our dog Tanner died only a few days later," Kristen Hayes-Yearick said. "Our veterinarian told us this toxic substance killed our dog, and our doctors said that it has caused profound health problems for our entire family."[19]

(HDPE), and a host of other resins used in packaging, plastic bags (including bottles labeled BPA-free), other plastics, and common fertilizers and pesticides all mimic estrogen.[17] These same chemicals have also been linked to potential male reproduction issues including low sperm counts, malformed genitalia, and increased frequency of non-descending testicles.[18]

All of us care that a baby is born healthy. No one wants to see a child born with his or her opportunities limited due to brain damage or other developmental problems. Nor do we wish to see our wives, sisters, daughters, and granddaughters face the plague of breast cancer. Yet one of the serious national failures has been to update the Toxic Substances Control Act (TSCA). This statute on the books, with no serious amendments since 1976, has in effect allowed over 85,000 chemicals to be marketed without serious testing; it also doesn't require combinations of chemicals to be tested.

As we write, there is legislation in Congress for TSCA reform known as the Frank R. Lautenberg Chemical Safety for the 21st Century Act, named for the late New Jersey senator who fought for years to update our chemical laws. Even if this compromised bill makes it through Congress, it fails to protect babies in the womb, the most vulnerable group. Unborn children—or the more popular politically correct term, developing fetuses—should be at the front of the line in efforts to update our chemical safety laws, but the Frank R. Lautenberg Chemical Safety for the 21st Century Act leaves this most vulnerable group out altogether. They're not just at "the back of the bus"— they're not even on the bus, left out in the cold as if they don't exist.

Strangely enough, in this era of rank partisanship, there seems to be bipartisan agreement to leave babies in the womb unprotected. But as a nation we cannot let political expediency and misplaced culture-war thinking leave babies in the womb unprotected from toxic chemicals that will damage them for the rest of their lives. Harvard professor Philippe Grandjean put it succinctly: "We only get one chance to develop a brain. The damage that occurs to the brain of a fetus or child will likely remain for the rest of his or her life."[20] The science is settled. The developing fetus and young child are particularly vulnerable to certain environmental toxins. Critical neurodevelopmental processes occur in the human central nervous system during fetal development and in the first three years of life.[21]

These issues should not be "politics as usual." The Environmental Protection Agency's (EPA) website lists over four thousand references to the "developing fetus," including a fact sheet on bioaccumulation of toxic chemicals that states, "The populations at risk . . . are children and the developing fetus."

Besides the critical neurodevelopment that occurs before birth, the other major reason babies in the womb are so vulnerable is bioaccumulation. Chemicals readily pass from the mother through the placenta; unfortunately, a developing baby, unlike the mother, cannot eliminate toxins through normal biological processes. In fact, one way chemicals are removed from a pregnant woman is by passing through her uterus.

Without explicitly including "developing fetuses" as a class to be protected, our most vulnerable population will continue to be exposed to chemicals that will substantially impact their entire lives and hinder our nation.

Yet Senate offices on both sides of the aisle refuse to consider adding the necessary language to protect our most at-risk population. Why? On one side, the chemical industry doesn't wish to acknowledge the reality of the impact their products have on babies in the womb, fearing it could lead to increased litigation, awarded damages, and more stringent testing that would impact their bottom line.

The other side says the term *developing fetus* veers too close a pro-life position—why, is beyond us, given its usage by scientists and the EPA—and they worry about their base. (Don't pro-choice individuals want children born healthy? Of course they do.) They are too happy including only "pregnant women," even though medical research clearly differentiates a pregnant woman from a developing fetus. I have been told that our concern for the "developing fetus" is a poison pill that would kill the proposed legislation. While the bill is marginally better than the 1976 law, it's terribly flawed.

Proponents on Capitol Hill have pointed out to us that the proposed legislation allows the EPA to name additional vulnerable populations. Such a provision is needed so that heretofore unknown vulnerable classes can be protected once science demonstrates their vulnerability. That does not apply here, given the settled science on the dangers toxic chemicals pose to babies in the womb. If the bill becomes law, it will exclude our most vulnerable and sadly reflect the state of our nation.

So on top of a world where we already poison our kids, climate change is adding insult to injury. As our temperature rises, smog will get worse—impacting those with asthma and making life more difficult. Dengue fever (known as bone-break fever for its pain), a mosquito-borne disease never before native to the U.S., is now present in Florida, Texas, and Hawaii, due at least in part to our changing climate and warming temperatures.[22] And in my home state of Pennsylvania, where we unfortunately lead the nation in Lyme disease infections, earlier springs and later autumn have made Lyme disease almost an epidemic.[23] Just recently, the Centers for Disease Control stated that the number of counties with high rates of Lyme disease, including counties in Pennsylvania, New York, Maryland, Connecticut, and Massachusetts, increased by more than 320 percent. Why? Climate change.[24]

Not only do the chemicals we spew into creation poison our kids, but our changing climate elevates food and water scarcity, causes increased extreme weather, and further taxes the resources needed to sustain 7.2 billion lives. One story that typifies the impacts comes from veterinarian, Christian missionary, and peacemaker Dr. Valery Shean.

Dr. Shean, a member of Christian Veterinary Mission, has worked in Uganda for over twenty years. Uganda, like much of Africa, is experiencing seasonal changes and decreased rainfall as climate change's impact deepens. The rainy season doesn't start on time, and rains come much more intermittently—and when they do, they come in much more rapid downpours than in the past. This exacerbates crop production, increases poverty, leads to starvation, and increases violence. It also leads to one of the most powerful stories I have ever heard.

Dr. Shean recounted the story of a young woman who was tossed away from her home by her husband. The woman's failure was that she couldn't grow a garden. Climate change's intermittent and altered rainfall pattern had led many in the area to have failed gardens. After several years of unsuccessful gardening, the young woman's husband cast her aside, blaming her for the garden's failure. She

Climate Change and One Developing Country

Like many other developing countries, Malawi has experienced a number of adverse climatic hazards. The most serious ones have been dry spells, seasonal droughts, intense rainfall, riverine floods, and flash floods. Some of these—especially droughts and floods—have increased in frequency, intensity, and magnitude over the same two decades, and have adversely impacted food and water security, water quality, energy, and sustainable livelihoods of the most rural communities.

Currently, the majority of rural communities in Malawi are experiencing chronic food deficits on a year-round basis owing to the effects of floods and droughts. . . . Erratic rains have resulted in acute crop failure, despite concrete efforts to improve seasonal weather forecasting at the beginning of the rainy season. Floods have also resulted in the disruption of hydroelectric power generation, water pollution, and increased incidence of diseases such as malaria, cholera, and diarrhea.[25]

fled to a nearby village, seeking shelter and security with another man. After becoming pregnant, the young woman was again tossed aside and became seriously ill. She made her way back to Dr. Shean, who cared for the woman and helped her deliver. Shortly after the birth, the woman died and Dr. Shean became the foster mother of what she calls her "Climate Baby."

Stories like Dr. Shean's are not uncommon—they happen every day as people struggle for food and water. We know that in Malawi, crops have decreased roughly a third from what had been produced in previous years. Our Malawian friends, the Assembly of God relief agency, tell us that for generations people would plant in late October or early November because they could predict the rainy season starting within a few days. While the total rainfall hasn't varied on a yearly basis, the rains now come months later and usually in extreme downpours, washing away the crops and the fields. By 2020, rain-fed farming will harvest only 50 percent of what they did just a few years ago across all Africa.[26]

It's not just food. Water remains the most precious life resource on earth. One billion people depend on melting glaciers for their water. The snows of Kilimanjaro have all but disappeared, the Andes (South America) glaciers are disappearing at an alarming rate, and the United States isn't being spared from water scarcity. Paul discussed the California and other western U.S. droughts, but if we open our eyes it's not hard to see the fouled water caused by our poor stewardship of creation. In the summer of 2014, we saw the city of Toledo's drinking water turn to slime as Lake Erie was filled with a gigantic algae bloom, fed by an exorbitant amount of petrochemicals (primarily fertilizer) and further escalated by higher water temperatures. The ensuing condition caused a massive panic. In Charleston, West Virginia, the Kanawha River became undrinkable from a coal preparation plant spill. And North Carolina saw a coal ash leak foul the Dan River, resulting in a $102 million fine and residents around the state wondering about the safety of their wells.[27]

Most of us remember the Deep Water Horizon oil spilled in the Gulf of Mexico in April 2010. Over 4.9 million barrels of crude oil spewed over at least eighty-seven days, making it the largest spill in United States history and recorded the largest fine of some $20 billion. Two surprising items continue to amaze me regarding the BP incident. First, the total amount of crude oil spilt represents only a little over six minutes of our daily use of petroleum in the United States, and while the impacts will continue for at least a generation, it's not the worst creation care threat to the Gulf of Mexico.

Each year, an average of five thousand square miles of Gulf water is dead. That's an area roughly equal to the size of Connecticut. The dead zones occur as an overabundance of fertilizer runs off farmland into the Mississippi River and becomes superfood for algae. The algae grows and consumes all the oxygen in the water, killing the remainder of marine life. Not only does this condition destroy the God-given balance, it results in an economic loss of some $2.8 billion to both commercial and recreational fishing.

There are over four hundred dead zones worldwide and over 166 identified in the United States, including parts of the Chesapeake Bay and Long Island Sound.[28] So, why should I care? First, much of the world's food, especially much-needed protein, comes from the oceans. Combined with overfishing, coral destruction, and other pollution, dead zones exacerbate food scarcity. This directly leads to increased levels of poverty, forced migration, and armed conflict. Second, oceans produce approximately 70 percent of the world's oxygen, and we all need to breathe. Expanding dead zones stress the created order and completely alter God's design for our common home.

We are easily fulfilling Isaiah's prophetic visions when he stated:

> The earth dries up and withers, the world languishes and
> withers,
> the heavens languish with the earth. The earth is de-
> filed by its people;

> they have disobeyed the laws, violated the statutes and
> broken the everlasting covenant. Therefore a curse
> consumes the earth; its people must bear their guilt.
> Therefore earth's inhabitants are burned up, and
> very few are left.
>
> Isaiah 24:4–6

The headlines are bad enough and highlight impotable water as a growing problem, but some might see these as unique and unrelated to our everyday life. Water is a matter of life, and all of us are at risk. I invite everyone to take a look at their local water quality. Every state has water advisories such as fish-eating limits because of mercury or agricultural waste petrochemicals. Water is key to our survival and yet we've polluted it so terribly. In the summer of 2015, it was revealed that thousands of bass with cancerous lesions have been seen in the Susquehanna River in my home of Pennsylvania with no definite answers why. It is certainly linked to our overuse of chemicals, our improper stewardship, and our failure to understand that we have been called to be stewards, not destroyers, of God's creation.

Ensuring pure water for all people would be considered a basic right for us in the United States. However, on a global scale, water resources are quickly becoming privatized. Privatization refers to water for those with the financial resources—not encompassing the general public.

Most of us would do anything to defend our kids. Without food, water, and hope, millions of people throughout the world are on the move, creating a new population group: climate refugees. In north Mexico alone, since the mid-1990s, over one million people have fled their farms each year due to poor farming conditions and climate change.[29]

"Today's refugee problem is perhaps a small indication of what the future will be like if we do not take action with respect to climate change," says billionaire Elon Musk, a socially conscious clean energy entrepreneur.[30] The mass immigration and refugee crises occurring in Europe and the flight of children to the United States from Latin America frame the issues that Musk highlights. While various organizations and researchers have attempted to quantify this new exodus, there is not common agreement on the actual migration; it's estimated to include somewhere between 50 and 200 million of God's children in the next several decades. While the numbers remain suspect, the impacts are not. The United States and Europe already face social unrest with the current wave of refugees, and climate change simply makes it worse.

Our military is concerned. They see climate change as a threat multiplier. I've sat in a room with retired generals and admirals from all branches of service and listened while, with moisture forming in their eyes, they shared their great fear of our nation committing our young men and women into conflict as more and more nations destabilize. I shared their tears as my eldest son served two tours in Afghanistan as a cavalry scout. In the last two Quadrennial Defense Reviews by the U.S. Department of Defense, climate risks were identified as follows:

> Climate change poses another significant challenge for the United States and the world at large. As greenhouse gas emissions increase, sea levels are rising, average global temperatures are increasing, and severe weather patterns are accelerating. These changes, coupled with other global dynamics, including growing, urbanizing, more affluent populations, and substantial economic growth in India, China, Brazil, and other nations, will devastate homes, land, and infrastructure. Climate change may exacerbate water scarcity and lead to sharp increases in food costs. The pressures caused by climate change will influence resource competition while placing additional burdens on economies, societies, and governance institutions around the world. These effects are threat multipliers that will aggravate stressors abroad such as poverty, environmental degradation, political instability, and social tensions—conditions that can enable terrorist activity and other forms of violence.[31]

Risks to Our National Security?

In many areas, the projected impacts of climate change will be more than threat multipliers; they will serve as catalysts for instability and conflict. In Africa, Asia, and the Middle East, we are already seeing how the impacts of extreme weather, such as prolonged drought and flooding—and resulting food shortages, desertification, population dislocation and mass migration, and sea level rise—are posing security challenges to these regions' governments. We see these trends growing and accelerating. To protect our national security interests both at home and abroad, the United States must be more assertive and expand cooperation with our international allies to bring about change and build resilience. The rapidly changing Arctic region is a clear example of where such international cooperation and change is imperative.[32]

Center for Naval Analyses Military Advisory Board

Climate change is resulting in war. I can almost hear the skeptical chuckles by some far-right political pundit on television—but have no doubt, while our changing of creation doesn't make war happen, the impacts are literally the powder keg waiting for a spark.

Stephen Faris, in *The Atlantic* magazine, tells the story of Alex de Waal, a graduate student who traveled in Sudan in the mid-1980s to assess the country's prolonged drought.[33] In de Waal's journeys he came across an older Arab sheikh named Hilal Abdalla, who said, "The God-given order was broken," and he feared the future. "The way the world was set up since time immemorial was being disturbed." Once, the mostly Arab nomads from northern Sudan coexisted with the primarily Christian farmers from the south. But as water and resource scarcity exacerbated, a civil war erupted, costing hundreds of thousands of lives and creating millions of refugees. The fact that that war is still ongoing is, in part, a result of climate change. No one will ever know what percentage of the Darfur conflict can be linked to climate change, but its one real example of why our military and researchers are concerned. Studies predict that each additional 1 degree Celsius or 1.8 degree Fahrenheit will result in a 20 to 49 percent increase in conflict in Africa alone.[34, 35]

Conservatives like Paul and I, and probably most of you reading this book, care about our families, our children, and our grandchildren. We want a strong America with a good economy. Our hope is to see children and grandchildren grow and thrive, with good jobs and a solid future. Our goal is pure air, clean water, and an unspoiled earth for an abundant, healthy life that allows them to reach their God-given potential. We desire their achievements to rely on sound faith, morals, and the Protestant work ethic instilled in us, not hindered in how ours and past generations soiled God's creation. We don't want the government to do it; we want to be able to accomplish something, and we want a sense of fairness where hard work is rewarded, where people are given equal opportunity to succeed in making that abundant life. In short, we desire America to bless God, and then God to bless America.

Overcoming climate change and our poor stewardship will require hard work. But before we tackle the very real problems, we first must break from our folly of polarization named in the beginning of this chapter. We need a third way to create a new future of America coming together. Perhaps its initiation was when a Christian leader visited the United States in September 2015.

For a coal miner's son from the little coal-mining town of Blandburg, Pennslyvania, I have experienced more than I ever imagined. I have gotten to travel the world, and since becoming the president of the Evangelical Environmental Network (EEN), I have had tea with the Prince of Wales, talked with the President of the United States, and learned to call the head of the Environmental Protection Agency a friend. I have developed great relationships with influential pastors and business leaders, but being part of Pope Francis's welcome to the White House in 2015 tops them all.

Standing on the South Lawn and watching the ceremony, the amazing grace of Jesus shined through a unique man. President Obama told Pope Francis, "In your humility, your embrace of simplicity, in the gentleness of your words and the generosity of your spirit, we see a living example of Jesus' teachings, a leader whose moral authority comes not just through words but also through deeds."

Since I am an evangelical Christian, Pope Francis is not the head of my church. But Pope Francis is perhaps the most important Christian leader of our generation simply because he is a living example of Jesus' teaching, guided by that shining grace.

Mercy, love, and hope shined through the brief welcoming ceremony. Perfect strangers chatted like old friends and people went out of their way to help each other. Shortly before the official start, a friend of mine, who also happened to be at the White House, ran into me and stood beside me. After a few minutes, he started to sway, and suddenly he collapsed in my arms. Before I could gently lay him on the ground, bystanders rushed to help. Some helped get him safely on the grass, others called out for a doctor, another rushed to the first aid tent, and several others formed a wide protective circle allowing the professionals to offer aid. Regardless of political party, not caring about race or religion, people helped a person in need.

While we acknowledged our differences, grace bridged them to create a sense of common purpose. It's a model for us as individuals, for our families, and for our state and national leaders. Far too often we are so devoid of grace we can find no common ground.

It's time to stop dehumanizing each other from within our ideological bastions and allow grace to shine through each of us, working for hope for all God's children and our common home. Pope Francis said, "We know by faith that the Creator does not abandon us; He never forsakes His loving plan or repents of having created us. Humanity has the ability to work together in building our common home."

Pope Francis's moral support for climate action stands together with the Orthodox Church, the Cape Commitment issued by the Lausanne Movement for World Evangelism, the National Association of Evangelicals, the Evangelical Climate Initiative, and most important, the Bible. May all of us search our hearts and look to see climate action in new ways with grace-filled eyes. For me, it's the greatest moral challenge of our generation and the greatest opportunity for hope. Climate change is the critical problem to solve, and with the solution comes the opportunity to defend our kids and create a new, better economy.

So let's quit building walls around our ideological positions and allow grace a chance to find common ground and help us work together.

CHAPTER 3

A Healthy Dose of Skepticism

Christians must care about climate change because we love God the Creator and Jesus our Lord, through whom and for whom the creation was made. This is God's world, and any damage that we do to God's world is an offense against God Himself.

National Association of Evangelicals

I do not feel obliged to believe that the same God who has endowed us with sense, reason, and intellect has intended us to forgo their use.

Galileo

God saw all that he had made, and it was very good.

Genesis 1:31

As human beings we are hardwired to react to weather. Maybe it's in our DNA, but when we look out the window, we naturally assume it's like this *everywhere*. Unless you can look out your window and see the entire planet (a pretty cool trick!), it's shortsighted to make global assumptions. Keeping a broad, global perspective is essential. Everything and everyone is interconnected.

We do, however, have a semantics challenge. When you hear "global warming," the impression is that it's warming up everywhere, all the time. Since we don't live on Venus, where a runaway greenhouse effect keeps the entire planet's surface a toasty 864 degrees F, this isn't an issue. *"But Paul, the climate has always been changing! How do we know this time is any different?"* From the standpoint of a bewildered meteorologist, rather than "global warming," I prefer the term "climate volatility" resulting in more "weather disruption." Doesn't exactly roll off the tongue, but it sums up the current state of affairs: more frequent and head-snapping swings of temperature and moisture; extremes trending more extreme.

Since the dawn of time we've experienced storms and weather extremes. But there's a growing body of evidence suggesting that heat-trapping greenhouse gas pollution from burning coal, oil, and gas, is already impacting weather patterns around the world. It's important to add that all these storms, droughts, and heat waves would have formed naturally, but a warmer atmosphere and warming oceans are amping up the effects of heat, drought, precipitation patterns, and sea level rise.

As a meteorologist, I'm the equivalent of a dermatologist, tracking the symptoms in day-to-day weather above the earth's skin. It's the climate scientists who are conducting the full-body CT scans, confirming that the patient is, in fact, running a low-grade fever.

Why trust the scientists? "They're just in it for the big grant money," people say. But wait. How many climate scientists are in the 1 percent driving Lamborghinis to the lab? The same men and women who could make far more money in the private sector but do their work because they love science? Is this a scam—a

SACRAMENTO—Brown lawns and stressed trees are a constant reminder for Californians that the state is in the midst of an historic four-year drought. This has been a real wake-up call about weather and climate. The infrastructure for water storage and delivery developed in the early 1900s may not meet the needs of a warmer and more heavily populated state. Now that Californians are being hit in the pocketbook, there's a greater sense of concern. One of the biggest questions heading into the winter season: Will the developing El Niño get us out of the drought? The answer is simple: It will only provide relief. If climate models are any indication, Californians will see more droughts like this.

Monica Woods, Chief Meteorologist, KXTV

brilliantly conceived swindle to advance a liberal agenda? A global conspiracy, involving thousands of independent scientists, researchers, and scientific organizations—a grand Machiavellian plot to grow government and take away our personal freedom? Think about it. Our government can't even launch a website.

"I read it on the Internet so it must be true!" Beware of conspiracy theories. When the facts and evidence aren't on their side, some people, institutes, special interests, and politicians addicted to a steady IV-drip of campaign donations find it easier to rely on conspiracy theories and manufactured misinformation. You're welcome to your opinions and beliefs—just not the facts. Even so, in a day and age of liberal media spin and slanted news, it's difficult to know who to trust and when.

"If Al Gore brought this issue to the public, it must be wrong!" Did Al Gore inadvertently politicize climate change by making his 2007 documentary, *An Inconvenient Truth?* Yes. His subsequent wealth and political activism, along with overzealous calls for crippling regulation and bigger government to solve the climate dilemma, has perpetuated the myth that climate change is a "liberal cause."

But thermometers and satellites don't have a political agenda. The data is the data—the facts are the facts.

Would we be debating the science if a conservative leader had stepped up? In late 2007, I had a chance to introduce one of my heroes, Senator John McCain, as we welcomed war veterans returning home from Iraq. I had the honor of sitting at his table during the event and I asked him a question that had been on my mind after seeing a new level of volatility on my weather maps: "Senator, could these changes in the climate be a fluke, a coincidence? Are we making too big a deal out of all this?" He rolled his eyes at me. "Paul, I'm seeing the changes in my home state of Arizona. I just got back from a trip to the Yukon, where a village elder presented me with a four-thousand-year-old tomahawk that had just melted out of the permafrost. No, this isn't a coincidence."

In 1863, Abraham Lincoln created the National Academy of Sciences (NAS), a private, nonprofit organization charged with providing independent, objective advice to the nation on matters related to science and technology. This was the height of the Civil War, and Lincoln, a Republican, was concerned about the military being scammed by shoddy contractors making unsubstantiated claims about their new inventions. He wanted a bipartisan group of scientific experts to evaluate these claims and make recommendations. In 2014, the very same NAS wrote:

> Climate change is one of the defining issues of our time. It is now more certain than ever, based on many lines of evidence, that humans are changing Earth's climate. The atmosphere and oceans have warmed, accompanied by sea-level rise, a strong decline in Arctic sea ice, and other climate-related changes. The evidence is clear. However, due to the nature of science, not every single detail is ever totally settled or completely certain.[1]

Science is never settled. As new observations are made and theories tested, science zigs and zags toward truth, however relative and

PHILADELPHIA—Warmest year. Warmest spring. Hottest summer. Most days of 90+ degrees. Hottest June. Hottest July. Wettest year. Wettest summer. Wettest single day. Wettest March. Wettest June. Wettest July. Wettest August. Snowiest winter. Snowiest month. Snowiest December. Snowiest February. Second and third biggest snowstorms. Lowest barometric pressure (Sandy). Official records in Philadelphia go back to 1871. That's 145 years. Yet all those above records happened in SIX! Ocean temperatures off the coast have been well above "normal" during Sandy and many of the other big, wet storms that led to these records. An enhanced greenhouse effect, caused mainly by an increase in CO_2, is known to lead to more "precipitable water" (PW). More PW in any given storm will likely lead to more precipitation. And, if it happens to be just cold enough, that means a bigger snowstorm. So, evidence of a "global warming effect" is already being seen in this area. Similar stories are being told elsewhere.

Glenn "Hurricane" Schwartz, Chief Meteorologist, NBC 10

impermanent. Science is a tool, a way of observing and measuring everything around us to create even better tools for our tool box. We didn't come out of the Stone Age because we ran out of stones. We came out of the Stone Age because we found a better way forward. "The New Testament talks about how faith is the evidence of things not seen," says Katharine Hayhoe, a Texas Tech climate scientist and evangelical Christian. "By definition, science is the evidence of things that are seen, that can be observed, that are quantifiable. And so that's why I see faith and science as two sides of the same coin."[2]

Personally, I believe in more than what I can observe and measure. There *are* absolutes, and our faith, which falls outside the scientific method, binds us to our Creator. But that doesn't mean we ignore 97 percent of climate experts, any more than we'd ignore 97 percent of cardiologists, teachers, or engineers. Four independent research studies all get the same results on the *overwhelming consensus*: 97 percent of climate specialists—people who devote their entire careers to tracking subtle, long-term changes—agree the planet is warming.

Despite the vast majority of studies, special interests are trying to convince the public that scientists are in disagreement. That's simply not the case. You can have an opinion, but that doesn't mean you're an expert, you're correct, or that the data supports

SEATTLE—The semi-reformed pirate Sir Francis Drake sneeringly referred to the Pacific Northwest as a land of "congealed rain," while a popular story of early Seattle focuses on a hat found in the midst of a muck-filled street. No one would touch the hat, it was explained, because they were afraid of who they might find buried beneath it. But the Northwest's reputation for wet, chilly weather has been endangered by major shifts the past few years. In 2015 alone, new records were set for the number of days exceeding both 80 and 90 degrees, and for nights that more closely resembled cities east of the Rockies. Mountains that routinely set records (world-records!) for annual snowfall were largely barren of snow by early summer, and glaciers on the massive volcanoes are shrinking. Tinder-dry vegetation ignited by lightning strikes or human carelessness have resulted in record wildfire seasons. The lack of snowmelt has also led to extremely low river levels and record warm water temperatures, which are endangering the survival of emerging salmon. Scientists have measured increasing levels of carbon dioxide mixing with sea water, which is sufficiently changing the chemistry through a process called *ocean acidification* to damage the shells of plankton, which support mature salmon—to say nothing of larger shellfish. From the mountains that pierce the sky and the inland seas that surround them, change is evident, and it's threatening the economic well-being of important segments in this growing region.

Jeff Renner, Chief Meteorologist (retired), KING-TV

your claims. We should listen to real experts and not look for conspiracy theories under every rock. "Science is not a democracy. It's a dictatorship. Evidence does the dictating," says John Reisman, director of the film *Climate Change: Lines of Evidence.*

Skepticism is a good thing. Scientists are skeptical by nature, and extremely competitive. For thousands of PhD professionals to agree on anything confirms that confidence levels are very high, even if we don't have every detail and the science isn't totally settled. But valid questions remain. Here are a few:

1. How do we know recent climate change is man-made? By taking careful measurements of the chemical composition of the atmosphere over time, we know that concentrations of carbon dioxide and other greenhouse gases have been increasing since the dawn of the Industrial Revolution.

> Since the mid-1800s, scientists have known that CO_2 is one of the main greenhouse gases of importance to Earth's energy balance. Direct measurements of CO_2 in the atmosphere and in air trapped in ice show that atmospheric CO_2 increased by about 40% from 1800 to 2012. Measurements of different forms of carbon isotopes reveal that this increase is due to human activities.[3]

Studies dating back to 1824 correctly identified the greenhouse gas effect. The steady rise in global surface temperature is consistent with the observed rise in CO2. These carbon dioxide "isotopes" are chemical fingerprints, proving man-made emissions and deforestation—not natural causes—are behind the spike in CO2.[4] History shows a tight correlation between carbon levels and the average temperature of the atmosphere. Again, there's nothing controversial about that statement.

CO2 traps warmth and keeps temperatures in a tolerable range for life to exist, but too much CO2 turns up the thermostat. There is an ideal range of carbon in the atmosphere. Oxygen is also essential for life; too much oxygen and things begin to spontaneously combust. As mentioned earlier, the concentrations of carbon in the atmosphere are higher than they've been since humans first walked the earth. We are conducting an experiment that's never been done before. A well-respected climate science site, Skeptical Science, confirms that actual observations nearly match what was predicted decades ago:

> An increased greenhouse effect would make nights warm faster than days, and this is what has been observed. If the warming is due to solar activity, then the upper atmosphere (the stratosphere) should warm along with the rest of the atmosphere. But if the warming is due to the greenhouse effect, the stratosphere should cool because of the heat being trapped in the lower atmosphere (the troposphere). Satellite measurements show that the stratosphere is cooling. This combination of a warming troposphere and cooling stratosphere should cause the tropopause, which separates them, to rise. This has also been observed. It was predicted that the ionosphere would shrink, and it is indeed shrinking.[5]

2. What role has the sun played? A good question, and one of the first inputs climate experts examined. Could fluctuations in the sun's energy be at least partly to blame for the observed warming over the last fifty years? Here's an excerpt from a series of very good explanations at The Royal Academy in the United Kingdom, the rough equivalent of our National Academy of Sciences:

> The Sun provides the primary source of energy driving Earth's climate system, but its variations have played very little role in the climate changes observed in recent decades. Direct satellite measurements since the late 1970s show no net increase in the Sun's output, while at the same time global surface temperatures have increased.[6]

It's not the sun, and it's not volcanoes either. The state of Florida emits more CO_2 every year than all the world's volcanoes.[7] In fact, it's estimated that volcanoes account for roughly 1 percent of the

Measurements of Surface Temperature and Sun's Energy

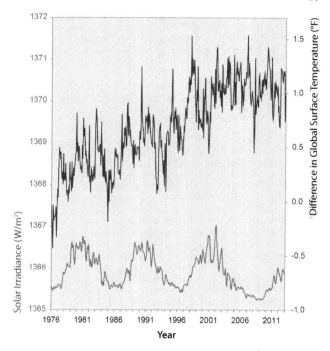

carbon released by burning fossil fuels every year to power our homes and vehicles.[8]

3. Climate is always changing. Why is climate change such a big deal now? Earth's climate has changed since the creation, responding to multiple inputs or "forcings"—wobbles in the earth's orbit, volcanoes, and slight variations in the amount of the sun's energy reaching our planet. It's the *rate* of change that concerns experts—how quickly we're releasing buried carbon back into the atmosphere:

CO2 has risen by 40% in just the past 200 years, contributing to human alteration of the planet's energy budget that has so far warmed Earth by about 0.8 °C (1.4 °F). If the rise in CO2 continues

WILKES-BARRE/SCRANTON—During the last thirty-five years of observing and predicting the weather for northeastern and central Pennsylvania, the most noticeable change I've seen is the afternoon high temperatures. They have trended roughly 5 degrees warmer from what I recall the first few years I lived here. In line with this, I've noticed fewer days with extremely cold temperatures in winter, not only at the airport but in many outlying areas. Also, our number of sub-zero days has been in decline. Finally, I've noticed a slight drop in our average seasonal snowfall, down about 4 inches from what I recall when I first moved here in 1981.

Tom Clark, Chief Meteorologist, WNEP-TV

unchecked, warming of the same magnitude as the increase out of the ice age can be expected by the end of this century or soon after.[9]

Earth's lower atmosphere is becoming warmer and moister as a result of human-emitted greenhouse gases. This gives the potential for more energy for storms and certain severe weather events. Consistent with theoretical expectations, heavy rainfall and snowfall events (which increase the risk of flooding) and heat waves are generally becoming more frequent. Trends in extreme rainfall vary from region to region: the most pronounced changes are evident in North America and parts of Europe, especially in winter.[10]

4. If the world is warming, why are some winters and summers still very cold? We experience weather every day, and big shifts in temperature often flavor our opinion of climate change. It's easier to acknowledge global warming during the summer. It's how we're wired. Due to positive feedbacks—melting polar ice and permafrost releasing methane, further accelerating the warming—the Arctic and latitudes near the poles are warming much faster than the rest of the planet.[11] This uneven warming may already be influencing the jet stream, creating a more volatile "high amplitude" pattern, one with bigger dips and bulges that favor more weather extremes. These gyrations in the steering winds can pull unusually cold air southward, even stalling weather patterns for weeks or months at a time. The Polar Vortex during the winter of 2013–2014 captured the imagination of the media, and ordinary Americans wondered (out loud) how a warming atmosphere could unleash such a blast of prolonged bitter air. The weather is more volatile, and even though the overall pattern is trending warmer, we'll still see outbreaks of frigid air. Again, a global perspective is required. Just because you're freezing doesn't mean the entire planet is in the deep freeze. Weather is local. Climate change is global. Keep an eye on the big picture.

Atmospheric and ocean circulation patterns will evolve as Earth warms and will influence storm tracks and many other aspects of the weather. Global warming tilts the odds in favor of more warm days and seasons and fewer cold days and seasons. For example, across the continental United States in the 1960s there were more daily record low temperatures than record highs, but in the 2000s there were more than twice as many record highs as record lows.

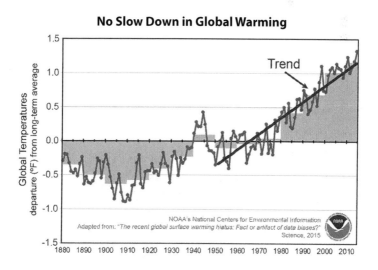

No Slow Down in Global Warming

65

Another important example of tilting the odds is that over recent decades heat waves have increased in frequency in large parts of Europe, Asia, and Australia.[12]

5. But I heard there hasn't been any warming in over fifteen years. Another popular meme, but the data just doesn't support the claim. NOAA and NASA data sets have improved over the years, and the latest data shows continued warming.[13] Keep in mind that nearly 92 percent of the extra warming triggered by greenhouse gases from burning fossil fuels goes into the world's oceans. Only 3 or 4 percent actually warms the atmosphere. El Niño and La Niña events in the Pacific can temporarily magnify or mask the broader trends.

Warming of the atmosphere, oceans, and cryosphere (icy regions of the planet) is uneven, but there is mounting evidence that the so-called "temperature hiatus," a speculative lull in the observed warming, was temporary and limited to the atmosphere while oceans continued to warm rapidly. It's the equivalent of going up a flight of steps and briefly catching your breath on the landing. It doesn't change the fact that you're climbing the stairs. No matter where you look—the oceans or the atmosphere—the earth is warming. Any claims that warming stopped fifteen years ago are false. Scientists have looked at the so-called pause. They can't find it.

6. How does climate change affect the strength and frequency of floods, droughts, hurricanes, and tornadoes? Severe weather attribution is emerging science. We don't yet have all the answers we need. There is strong evidence a warming climate is fueling longer, deeper heat waves and droughts worldwide. Confidence levels are high that a warmer, wetter atmosphere is fueling warmer nights and more intense summer season rains, capable of extreme flooding. The link to severe storms, tornadoes, and hurricanes is more tenuous, but there's little doubt that changing the chemical

COLUMBIA, SOUTH CAROLINA—The effects of a warmer earth can be observed even in South Carolina. Temperatures have not warmed as fast as other parts of the country, but there has still been an impact. The growing season has lengthened by about one week since 1970. At first glance this might seem like a good development, but it has allowed invasive insects to damage crops. Plant diseases are more common and harder to control. The rise in carbon dioxide has resulted in higher pollen counts and more toxic poison ivy over the past half century. Warmer temperatures are also allowing more water vapor into the atmosphere. This has led to an increased frequency in heavy downpours. In addition, the higher humidity in the summer is leading to higher heat indices. Low temperatures at night are warmer because of the moister atmosphere. As of 2015 the three hottest summers on record had occurred in the last six years. Those three summers were not the hottest by high temperatures, but each were the top three warmest by low temperatures. The combination of heat and humidity is beginning to affect crops dependent on pollen fertilization. Pollen's effectiveness decreases beyond certain temperatures. For example, corn needs daytime temperatures to remain below 95°F while tomatoes need nighttime temperatures to drop below 75°F to be effective. As the weather changes, the climate does too, and the impacts begin to build over time.

Jim Gandy, Chief Meteorologist, WLTX-TV

composition of the atmosphere may have more unpleasant, unintended side effects we didn't see coming.

7. Meteorologists can't even get the seven-day outlook right. Why should I trust a fifty-year climate outlook? A valid point. One that hurts my feelings, but meteorologists hear this all the time. It's comparing apples and oranges. Weather is chaotic and seemingly random. Meteorologists attempt to predict how the fluid of air overhead will move over time. We look at current data and scores of weather models, each one using slightly different math and physics to simulate what the atmosphere *should* look like at some specific point in the future. Weather forecasts are consistently wrong because we can't yet access a perfect snapshot of the atmosphere: the current data that fuels the models. The math that powers our models is only an approximation of reality. It's a model, and all models eventually fail. Frustrating? Absolutely. You have no idea. Weather forecasts have gotten better, but they'll never be perfect, in spite of Doppler radar, supercomputers, and fleets of weather satellites orbiting overhead.

WASHINGTON, D.C.—Every time we awake and begin a new day, we know the world around us is different. We are a day older, the weather, the news, what will happen the next minute, next hour, this new day, is different than any day we have lived before. Whatever our beliefs, our faith, we are unique life on the earth. We are aware of the changes around us, within our lives. The magic of star-filled night skies diminishes as night skies are ever brighter, the azure blue and clear waters of our childhood horizons and memories are muddled with "stuff." Weather changes. Weather is change, but we now have fewer cold days when our nose tingles, fewer snowy days when diamond crystals crunch. Cities are hotter in summer, storms are stronger, dry spells are longer, nights are warmer—maybe not terrible in winter but sure "different than the weather I remember." We love where we live, we love the ebb and flow of weather, water, our sky, the seasons, the rainy days, the sunny days, the cold days, the snowy days, the hot days, the special "school is canceled" because of weather days. We love it all. Let's not love it to death so our grandchildren can only imagine from our old tales of what this all was once like.

Bob Ryan, Consulting Meteorologist; Past President, American Meteorological Society

Even though meteorologists can't tell you whether a specific day next month will be warmer or colder than today, we sure know that July is warmer than January. Short-range forecasts are different from longer-term trends. Our climate responds to a wide range of inputs: orbital changes, fluctuations in the sun's energy reaching the surface, volcanoes and aerosols, natural and man-made pollutants. Climate models capture all these forcings, mapping out the broader trends. If CO_2 levels go up, temperatures warm, as they have since the creation. No other external factor better explains the temperature rise of the atmosphere and oceans—the things we're observing all around us. But this time *we* are the ones with our foot on the pedal. More warmth and energy is now showing up in the increasingly erratic weather rattling your rooftop.

The evidence is visible all around us. Cherry-picking data to make a point—or relying on intellectually lazy conspiracy theories—isn't an honest way to address the problem. The reality: Burning fossil fuels has powered economies and lifted much of the world out of abject poverty, but it has some very unpleasant side effects. We've gone from secondhand smoke to secondhand CO_2. Dirty fuels are compromising earth's natural checks and balances. The future is uncertain, but there's no time for doom and gloom. There *is* a way forward, one that cleans up our skies, improves our health, and leaves our kids a world we won't have to apologize for—a sustainable economic path that honors God's creation while creating new opportunities for renewal, rebirth, and reinvention. American exceptionalism? Let's prove it—again.

What if the vast majority of scientists, research papers, and predictions are right? We honor our Creator by keeping an open mind, by acknowledging that our actions have very real consequences on his creation. Anything less is the definition of apathy, indifference, and greed.

We need to pay attention.

Here's a forecast with a high degree of certainty. At some point your kids or grandkids will come to you and ask, "What did you know, when, and what did you do?" Did you sit on your hands, latch on to conspiracy theories, and kick the can down the road?

Or were you part of the solution?

CHAPTER 4

We Are . . .
Easter People

Dominion doesn't mean doing what you want. It means caring for what's been given to you in a healthy way.

Eugene Peterson

The majority of American evangelicals have experienced God in nature. Whether at Christian camp or on a hike in the wild, we've had a "mountaintop" encounter. The Evangelical Sisterhood of Mary in Phoenix, Arizona, were so moved by the majesty of the Grand Canyon that they placed three bronze plaques along the canyon's South Rim in the late 1960s. Although the tablets were the subject of some controversy a decade ago, I (Mitch) challenge anyone who has witnessed the great canyon not to think of God. In over five hundred sermons or presentations in churches across America in the past six years, I received nearly 100 percent affirmation when I asked, "How many have encountered Jesus in nature?"

It's almost incredulous that we meet God *in* creation but haven't made the connection that caring *for* creation nurtures our relationship with him. Creation care is a part of loving God. Throughout the Christian and Hebrew Scriptures, the Bible clearly states that the entire world, all creation, belongs to God, and we (humans) are stewards or caretakers of this marvelous and wonderful creation. As the Rev. Dr. Christopher Wright states in his seminal work, *The Mission of God*, we cannot have a relationship with God if we fail to care for what belongs to him.

And if the greatest commandment is that we should love God, that surely implies that we should treat what belongs to God with honor, care and respect. This would be true in any human

We love the world of God's creation. This love is not mere sentimental affection for nature (which the Bible nowhere commands), still less is it pantheistic worship of nature (which the Bible expressly forbids). Rather it is the logical outworking of our love for God by caring for what belongs to him. "The earth is the Lord's and everything in it." The earth is the property of the God we claim to love and obey. We care for the earth, most simply, because it belongs to the one whom we call Lord.

The earth is created, sustained and redeemed by Christ. We cannot claim to love God while abusing what belongs to Christ by right of creation, redemption and inheritance. We care for the earth and responsibly use its abundant resources, not according to the rationale of the secular world, but for the Lord's sake. If Jesus is Lord of all the earth, we cannot separate our relationship to Christ from how we act in relation to the earth. For to proclaim the gospel that says 'Jesus is Lord' is to proclaim the gospel that includes the earth, since Christ's Lordship is over all creation. Creation care is thus a gospel issue within the Lordship of Christ.[2]

The Cape Town Commitment, 2011

relationship. If you love someone, you care for what belongs to that person.

To love God (even to know God at all, Jeremiah would add [Jer. 9:24]) means to value what God values. Conversely, therefore, to contribute to or collude in the abuse, pollution and destruction of the natural order is to trample on the goodness of God reflected in creation. It is to devalue what God values, to mute God's praise and to diminish God's glory.[1]

When speaking at a church or Christian college, one of my favorite methods to demonstrate the creation care (stewardship) and God relationship is to invite two folks seated together to join me. I ask one of them if I can borrow their smartphone or tablet. I give the device to the other enlistee and then ask them what the first person would think if the second one threw the phone on the ground and stomped on it. Do they think they would remain friends? Simultaneously, with a bit of sleight of hand, I pull an old cell phone out of my pocket, throw it on the ground, and jump on it. With a surprised face and the look of hope that it wasn't my phone, I ask, "Could they be friends after something they owned was destroyed by the other?" There is always wide-eyed amazement, sometimes a nervous chuckle or even outright glares of hostility. I then repeat the question: *Would you be friends with me or with anyone who destroyed something that belonged to you?* Some attempt to provide a churchy answer like, "If you're sorry or if you buy me a new phone . . ." But the relationship is broken. Without some type of reconciliation and forgiveness, the brokenness continues. So, in part, our relationship with God is influenced by how each of us cares for his creation.

Christianity, above all else, is a faith built on relationship. The relationship existing between the Trinity (Father, Son, and Holy Spirit) is the ideal model. It's the relationship offered from the God who walked among his creation in the garden, to the God who heard, saw, and felt the cruelties heaped upon the Israelites in ancient Egypt, to the God in Jesus who became human to walk with us and then bore our blunders to restore our relationship. The Bible's central message remains God's love for us and God's work to restore our relationship. It is simply impossible to follow Christ, be a disciple, and have a complete relationship with God without caring for his creation. Yet far too many Christians are not practicing care for what God values.

Some time ago, I led a Harrisonburg community men's morning Bible study in Virginia. The lesson was based on Colossians 1:16–20:

> For in him all things were created: things in heaven and on earth, visible and invisible, whether thrones or powers or rulers or authorities; all things have been created through him and for him. He is before all things, and in him all things hold together. And he is the head of the body, the church; he is the beginning and the firstborn from among the dead, so that in everything he might have the supremacy. For God was pleased to have all his fullness dwell in him, and through him to reconcile to himself all things, whether things on earth or things in heaven, by making peace through his blood, shed on the cross.

The morning's key verse: "For in him all things were created: things in heaven and on earth, visible and invisible, whether thrones or powers or rulers or authorities; all things have been created through him and for him." This Scripture, like so many others in the Bible, tells Christians that we are not the owners of the earth. The earth, God's creation, was formed by and for God, for Jesus. Unfortunately, too many Christians, especially evangelicals, don't understand the imperative to "tend the garden."[3]

As a case in point, immediately after sharing, I sat down for a time of reflection and discussion. As soon as I was seated, one gentleman said, "I've read the Bible all my life, and I never saw this Scripture in the light of caring for the earth."

Christian earth stewardship or creation care, in my experience, is not a matter of willful disregard for the earth, but a matter of biblical ignorance. Much of evangelical Christianity, in the past, has been based in a platonic worldview.[4] What I mean by this is we've been taught that the only real thing is heaven; earthly reality exists only as a shade of the ideal. Therefore our vision, dreams, and theology have been based in saving souls and escaping the earth instead of its reconciliation and restoration. Since the return of a neo-orthodox theology after World War I, Lesslie Newbigin's book, *The Open Secret*, was the first to challenge this escapism theology.[5] Not surprisingly, Newbigin's work focuses on a passage similar to Colossians 1:

> In him we have redemption through his blood, the forgiveness of sins, in accordance with the riches of God's grace that he lavished on us. With all wisdom and understanding, he made known to us the mystery of his will according to his good pleasure, which he purposed in Christ, to be put into effect when the times reach their fulfillment—to bring unity to all things in heaven and on earth under Christ.
>
> Ephesians 1:7–10

Both Ephesians and Colossians provide us with the image that Jesus is the reconciler of all things, not just humanity. The whole of creation is to be healed through and by Jesus the Christ. It's not escaping the earth into heaven but heaven coming to earth[6] and the return to the beauty of the created order: the old becoming new, being the fulfillment of the kingdom. Jesus calls us to restore his will—his kingdom—on earth as it is in heaven. It's a return, quite honestly, to the beginning, to the garden of Eden in which we were called to live in harmonious relationship with the rest of creation, not destroy it.

As an evangelical Christian, the scriptural understanding of reconciliation comes through and by the resurrection of Jesus. In the gospel of John, chapter 20:1–18, Mary Magdalene comes to the garden tomb. Mary is lost, grieving, and alone in her own thoughts. The old gospel hymn "In the Garden" captures the intent of the Scriptures.

> I come to the garden alone,
> While the dew is still on the roses,

And the voice I hear falling on my ear
The Son of God discloses.
And He walks with me, and He talks with me,
And He tells me I am His own;
And the joy we share as we tarry there,
None other has ever known.[7]

Most of us know John's account of the resurrection. After finding the empty tomb, Mary runs and tells the other disciples that Jesus' body is gone and fears that it was stolen. Following the disciples back to the garden, Mary sees a stranger she presumes to be the gardener, the caretaker. She asked, "Where have you taken the body?" and the man simply replies, "Mary."

In that moment, Mary sees the risen Jesus. Joy and excitement replace her grief. She rushes over and tries to grab hold of Jesus, but he brushes her aside. Jesus doesn't allow Mary to grab hold of him, to cling to our Risen Lord. For most of my life and I'm sure for many other Christians, Jesus resisting Mary seems confusing, unloving, or even cruel. However, thanks to N. T. Wright, we have new insights into both Jesus and Mary.[8]

Mary, more than anything else, desired to cling to the Jesus that she knew. The Jesus who spent time with her, the Jesus who performed miracles, the Jesus who taught about love and forgiveness. In short, Mary wanted to cling to the past and not move into a new creation, the kingdom of God. So many of us are just like Mary. We don't want to change; we want to live in the past, or at least live where we are comfortable.

It's probably a bit oversimplified, but in the majority of the Western world, Christians live more like Good Friday Christians than Easter people. What do I mean? We, those of us among the dwindling number who count ourselves as Christian, like the concept that Jesus' death on the cross paid for our sins and wiped our slates clean. We love to have our mistakes taken care of so that we can get into heaven, but we really don't want to change our ways.

Accepting Jesus as Savior, for many, becomes the culmination of faith, instead of the beginning. We don't want to be part of a new creation. We really don't want to live our lives any differently. We are comfortable with who we are, and being something new is terribly disconcerting; it's enough to believe and not act like Jesus.

Those are my conclusions after almost twenty years as a local church pastor. Even on Easter—the last holy day not overtaken by our "stuff-driven" world—most people come to Easter services wanting to see an empty tomb, not experience a risen Savior. That's why Mary attempted to hold on to Jesus, but Jesus had other ideas. Jesus tells Mary not to hang on to the past, but to go and tell his disciples that he is going ahead of them into Galilee and he wants them to follow.

Understand that Paul and I are both Pennsylvania natives. While I fled from home to attend the University of Arizona, Paul graduated from Penn State University and remains part of its Meteorological Advisory Board. Paul now lives in the Twin Cities of Minnesota, while I returned to Pennsylvania. In addition to our faith and our concern for addressing climate change, we share another love: Penn State football. We have attended games together with our wives at Beaver Stadium, jumping, clapping, and cheering as loudly as the current students. From growing up near State College and being lifelong fans, we know the classic Penn State cheer: "We are Penn State." In fact, anywhere you go throughout the Commonwealth of Pennsylvania and someone says, "We are . . ." you know the reply will be "Penn State!"

I tell this aside as we in the church must decide what kind of Christians we are. Do we wish to remain Good Friday Christians, awaiting the escape of this world, or do we want to have a complete relationship with and follow our risen Lord Jesus? Are we willing to experience abundant life through Jesus, here and now, being part of the new creation, working with Jesus? Instead of a Penn State cheer, I have long desired the American church to respond after "We are" with "Easter People!" Are we willing to be the hands and feet of Jesus until he returns? The church's answer to the Resurrection, the Easter message, will determine the lives and future for literally hundreds of millions in our nation and throughout the world. Simply put, the future of American churches depends on our becoming Easter people.

Churches are losing many from the current generation. Why? Because many younger people, including some of my children, see no relevance in the church. They're not looking for heaven; they want a better world. But all they're seeing is an institution trying to preserve itself through the current culture wars; pointing fingers, hating, and especially not being filled with love or mercy. Secular humanism appears much more loving than the church to so many today.

There's a huge difference in how the current North American church loves and how Jesus loves. The first evangelist wasn't a perfect person but a woman who met Jesus at a well and, to say the least, had a complicated life. Or the Roman centurion's servant, healed by faith, who didn't have the correct form of baptism or even follow Jewish law. All of the disciples were flawed, ordinary people who, after experiencing the resurrection, finally started the transformation process. Christianity believes we can't do it alone. It's Jesus' love, given through grace, provided by the Holy Spirit, that takes us beyond ourselves.

Jesus' greatest command is "Love each other as I have loved you."[9] His love means for us to stop worrying about who gets into heaven and start building the kingdom of God on earth. Heaven is the icing on the spiritual journey, not the first priority. People struggling to live and breathe today are the priority. Jesus talked about the kingdom more than any other subject; even the Lord's Prayer's first petition after acknowledging the Holy Otherness of

God, requests, "Thy will be done on earth as in heaven." Building the kingdom is primary to the love of Christ, and our first priority is caring for the poor and broken in the world. Climate change impacts every single person on earth, from a tick-bitten boy in Pennsylvania to a five-year-old girl in Malawi who walks twelve miles a day for water.

Back in 2010, the EEN team helped me organize a three-hundred-plus-mile journey from Amsted, West Virginia, to Washington, D.C. Called the Creation Care Walk, we started at the home of a wonderful group called Christians for the Mountains. CFTM, led by Allen Johnson, works hard to limit the damage from mountaintop coal mining, including pollution in thousands of miles of streams. This team of primarily volunteers focuses on the health impacts caused by the destruction of the mountains, but I have never seen more Christian love as they work together for the future of West Virginia's miners and those impacted by various environmental health threats.

The idea for our Creation Care Walk started after reading a story of a young Malawian girl. This rural child, just five years old at the time, walked two round trips, totaling around twelve miles each day, to fetch water for her family. In many places, including Malawi, due to the combination of forest loss and changing rainfall (caused by both climate change and poor stewardship factors), it's more difficult to gather wood for fuel and to secure water. And in many rural cultures, women are responsible for water, fuel, farming, and child rearing. As women search farther and longer for fuel and water, violence potential increases, including rape, abduction, and even murder.[10] The violence is perhaps why the family selected the young girl, as she was considered the "least valuable."

This real-life tale broke my heart, and God called me to walk in her shoes, to tell her story and the ways climate challenges are already impacting God's kids. So we walked about fifteen miles each day, stopping at evangelical churches most nights to tell the story and sleep on their floor. When our team arrived in D.C., we prayed before our Capitol, calling our nation to quit using climate change as a political football and address it as the true matter of life and death that it is.

Matthew 25 instructs us to "care for the least of these." Micah tells us to walk humbly after our God. The Bible is clear and simple: We're to love as God loves, and we must care and empower the poor. Our changing climate simply makes Jesus' command harder. *The Lancet*, a leading medical journal, states that climate change "threatens to undermine the last half century of gains in development and global health."[11]

So. Let's roll up our sleeves and be Jesus' disciples.

> For it is by grace you have been saved, through faith—and this is not from yourselves, it is the gift of God—not by works, so that no one can boast. For we are God's handiwork, created in Christ Jesus to do good works, which God prepared in advance for us to do.
>
> Ephesians 2:8–10

For much of the church's history, we stopped reading this passage after "so that no one can boast." But we *have* been created to do good works, the work of God and his kingdom, as we await the return of Jesus and its completion.

Church-based relief and development organizations like World Relief, Food for the Hungry, and World Vision have for decades worked in compassion ministries. However, we need more than compassion; we need a transformation of the church.

Have you ever wondered why God doesn't just immediately take us to heaven the moment we accept his grace? Why does he leave us in a fallen world? He leaves us here to fulfill his purposes.[12]

Rick Warren

There are glimmers of hope. The Vineyard Movement, which recently started i-61, taken from Isaiah 61; the Kingdom Vision Church; International Justice Mission (IJM), which does outstanding ministry in rallying young people against human trafficking; our friends Jesus People Against Pollution, who fight environmental justice; and Mission America, the United States' arm of The Lausanne Movement, who launched Love 2020, asking every Christian to love another person so that the entire American population may experience Christ's love. I believe the world needs Jesus, and it's critically important that the church be Jesus for the world.

I often travel by air for speaking engagements or meetings as part of the Evangelical Environmental Network's ministry, and I usually sit in the window seat of a lower-cost airline. As the usually booked aircraft fills with passengers, it's not uncommon for a younger adult to be stuck in the center seat. At some point during the flight, the subject of professions comes up. When I reply that I am an evangelical environmentalist, the response is usually, "What are you talking about? There isn't such a person!"

With a captive and curious individual, I share the Scriptures; tell how we have a responsibility to steward God's creation and care for the least of these. I share Jesus' biblical call to love and make a better world here and now. Many never knew that there are evangelicals who care for the same issues many young adults care about—or even that we go beyond getting people "saved." But as people learn about Jesus and his love for all creation, they want to know more. The best part of the story: On several dozen occasions, they've made a commitment to follow Jesus.

Following our Risen Lord to Galilee and beyond calls for trust, faith, and an idea of the way. Fortunately for us, the Bible is the best guide to understanding the Bible, and perhaps the easiest way is to return to Jesus' resurrection as told in John's gospel.

"To Every Person Living on This Planet"

"Praise be to you, my Lord." In the words of this beautiful canticle, Saint Francis of Assisi reminds us that our common home is like a sister with whom we share our life and a beautiful mother who opens her arms to embrace us. "Praise be to you, my Lord, through our Sister, Mother Earth, who sustains and governs us, and who produces various fruits with colored flowers and herbs."

This sister now cries out to us because of the harm we have inflicted on her by our irresponsible use and abuse of the goods with which God has endowed her. We have come to see ourselves as her lords and masters, entitled to plunder her at will. The violence present in our hearts, wounded by sin, is also reflected in the symptoms of sickness evident in the soil, in the water, in the air and in all forms of life. This is why the earth herself, burdened and laid waste, is among the most abandoned and maltreated of our poor; she "groans in travail" (Rom. 8:22). We have forgotten that we ourselves are dust of the earth (cf. Gen. 2:7); our very bodies are made up of her elements, we breathe her air and we receive life and refreshment from her waters.[13]

Pope Francis

The majority of biblical scholars recognized long ago that John's garden resurrection provides powerful images of Jesus and his mission, building a new creation. As with the first creation, Adam is formed from the dust of the earth, and Jesus becomes the new or second Adam arising from a tomb buried in the dirt. Mary sees Jesus as a gardener, one who tends and cares for the creation. The gardener was the role the first Adam was to play, and above all, Jesus' resurrection takes place on the eighth day, or the first day of the new creation. The new creation has been symbolized for centuries with baptismal fonts constructed with eight sides. These biblical clues guide us directly back to the beginning, or more aptly, a new Genesis.

Thanks be to Jesus, we have been given a do-over, a continuing opportunity for a second chance for all life and caring for creation. We have a choice to follow Jesus from the garden and assist building this, his new creation, or grasping on to the past. Let's take a look at what was supposed to be, to live as disciples.

In the beginning, God created the heavens and the earth. We all know the opening verse of the Bible, but how many of us take to heart those words, "God created"? How long have we ignored God's ownership? "The heavens are yours, and yours also the earth; you founded the world and all that is in it."[14]

God's original creation was indeed very good. One look at the Bible reveals the design cast by the Holy Spirit roaming above the primeval earth. Sustainable life for all creation in relationship with the Creator flows from the Genesis narrative. The spoken word provided holistic life for each member of creation. Order existed. Life thrived, and all was good.

> Then God said, "I give you every seed-bearing plant on the face of the whole earth and every tree that has fruit with seed in it. They will be yours for food. And to all the beasts of the earth and all the birds in the sky and all the creatures that move along the ground—everything that has the breath of life in it—I give every green plant for food." And it was so.
>
> Genesis 1:29–30

Being fair, while humanity was first called to be vegetarians, those of us who enjoy meat can thank God for Genesis 9, where meat is put on the table.

> Then God blessed Noah and his sons, saying to them, "Be fruitful and increase in number and fill the earth. The fear and dread of you will fall on all the beasts of the earth, and on all the birds in the sky, on every creature that moves along the ground, and on all the fish in the sea; they are given into your hands. Everything that

lives and moves about will be food for you. Just as I gave you the green plants, I now give you everything.

Genesis 9:1–3

Competition for food and other resources never occurred as God provided all means for abundant life, and clearly, the patristic church leaders understood the message of a good creation.

Yet it was not because of its utility to him that he produced anything that exists, since being self-sufficient he is in need of nothing. It was rather out of his loving-kindness and goodness that he created everything; accordingly he created things in sequence and provided us with a clear instruction about created things through the tongue of the blessed author, so that we might learn about them precisely and not fall into the error of those led by purely human reasoning. [15]

God created the perfect place. Sometimes one catches brief glimpses of Eden in the world today. Perhaps in a beautiful sunset or a mountain stream, a baby's cry, or even the meter of a wonderful poem. Gerard Manley Hopkins, a nineteenth-century English priest, captures both the goodness as well as the ugliness after humanity's fall.

God's Grandeur

THE WORLD is charged with the grandeur of God
It will flame out, like shining from shook foil;
It gathers to a greatness, like the ooze of oil
Crushed. Why do men then now not reck his rod?
Generations have trod, have trod, have trod;
And all is seared with trade; bleared, smeared with toil;
And wears man's smudge and shares man's smell: the soil
Is bare now, nor can foot feel, being shod.
And for all this, nature is never spent;
There lives the dearest freshness deep down things;
And though the last lights off the black West went

Oh, morning, at the brown brink eastward, springs—
Because the Holy Ghost over the bent
World broods with warm breast and with ah! bright
  wings.[16]

Gerard Manley Hopkins (1877)

We have been given a precious gift, a planet that can provide for all our needs if we follow God and use it wisely. Just as we are called to love our neighbor, not subjugate him or her, the same applies to creation. We may not simply do as we please. How did we ever assume the earth was to be trashed or misused in any way? Genesis reports just the opposite. The earth supplies the necessities for biological life; God designed creation for exactly that purpose. God created and was the first gardener. For life to prosper, humans are to empower the garden to flourish. We have been clearly given the responsibility, as created in God's image, to reflect his image, God's presence, by caring for creation.

Unfortunately, many read the Bible from our fallen condition instead of the new creation offered in and through Christ. For by reading in our brokenness, we misread the text and examine it through our eyes instead of God's. One of the most widely misunderstood verses in the Bible comes in Genesis 1:28. Whether we use *subdue, dominate, rule,* or any of a host of English words, it conjures mental images of the right to do as we please without regard. Yes, the church has made a mistake in teaching some variation of this for much of its first two millennia. These are the same mistakes and rationalizations made regarding slavery or even the feudal system. Far too often we examine Holy Scripture looking up through our sin instead of down through God's grace.

The sad reality is that our stewardship reflects our relationship with God. Upon a close reading of Genesis 3, we understand that original sin was the temptation to be godlike, to be in control. Looking back at human history, our principal failing always seems to be the desire to be in charge, combined with the inability to live within God-given limits. The Genesis account describes a universal order with God as the loving and very good creator, humans cast in his image as partners in maintaining creation, and all creation living in a sustainable relationship.

Our desire to be in control, however, breaks the order, attempts to bypass the limits, and injures our relationship with God, leading to a broken and unsustainable world. Each time we use more than we need or consume greater than our share, we perpetuate our brokenness, support our vanity, and continue disregarding God's limits. This distorts the creation and impacts all.

Throughout the Old Testament, God defines and provides deliberate instructions for tending the earth. Although most Christians haven't made the connection, the Bible provides definitive mandates to love in relationship with the creation. In what I jokingly regard as the most-often read biblical books, Deuteronomy, Numbers, and Leviticus, God gives clear instruction for Sabbath rest, indications of crop rotation, and animal husbandry. There are strict ordinances regarding farming, livestock management, and land use in general.[17] These conditions define the parameters for living in relationship with God, people, and the earth in an integrated approach to life.

> If you follow my decrees and are careful to obey my commands, I will send you rain in its season, and the ground will yield its crops and the trees their fruit.
>
> Leviticus 26:3–4

In his centuries'-old commentary of Isaiah 24, John Calvin stated it best:

> There is a kind of mutual bargain between the land and the husbandmen, that it gives back with usury what it has received: if it does not, it deceives those who cultivate it. But he assigns a reason, imputing blame to them, that they render it barren by their wickedness. It is owing to our fault that it does not nourish

us or bring forth fruit, as God appointed to be done by the regular order of nature; for he wished that it should hold the place of a mother to us, to supply us with food; and if it change its nature and order, or lose its fertility, we ought to attribute it to our sins, since we ourselves have reversed the order which God had appointed; otherwise the earth would never deceive us, but would perform her duty.[18]

Disregarding God's instructions to tend and care for the earth results in the earth's failure to provide the necessities for sustaining life. Poor stewardship and our over-consumption utterly disregard the natural order. This is not just a matter of creation care, but of people care. The interdependent relationship between the earth, God's people, and all creation, bound together since the beginning, is failing because of humanity's inability to follow God's covenant.

I have often quipped and tweeted that if God wasn't a forgiving landlord, humanity would have been evicted long ago. Humanity has filled our common home with poison; we have given the earth a fever, in the words of my colleague Jim Ball.[19]

Paul has shared extensively how carbon pollution has, is, and will continue to heat up the earth. Proclamations of "the hottest year" pile up, but the most alarming fact is that we have not lived a month below the twentieth-century average temperature since February 1985. Ronald Reagan was president and one of my sons had yet to be born. However, it's not too late to change, thanks be to God. We simply have to remember:

> All the ends of the earth
> will remember and turn to the Lord,
> and all the families of the nations
> will bow down before him,
> for dominion belongs to the Lord
> and he rules over the nations.
>
> Psalm 22:27–28

Life is messy; there is a lot on our plates. But life for all creation can get better. It begins with acknowledging God is in charge. Without the hope of faith, I would be despondent. I couldn't live life without knowing Jesus and accepting the abundant life given through grace. I am convinced that the biblical way to ensure life to the fullest requires a complete relationship with Jesus: by knowing him and following his lead into his kingdom by doing the good works that he set before us. A huge part of discipleship means caring for what belongs to God and cherishing what God cherishes. It's the combination of knowing and doing that results in the peace, love, and joy promised as spiritual fruit by Paul in Galatians. Even if you question my theology about the end times, Jesus commands us not to be concerned about when, but do the work he has called each of us to now.

Creation care is a matter of life for our kids and, most important, part of a whole life in Christ. My prayer is that each of us walks with Jesus and follows his lead into his kingdom and his new creation.

CHAPTER 5

A Place for Faith and Science

A good person leaves an inheritance for their children's children, but a sinner's wealth is stored up for the righteous.

Proverbs 13:22

We need to move past debating and focus on the poorest of the poor who are neither scientists nor politicians but are the most affected by how we care for God's creation.

Leith Anderson, President of the National Association of Evangelicals

I say the Earth belongs to each generation during its course, fully and in its own right, and no generation can contract debts greater than may be paid during the course of its own existence.

Thomas Jefferson, 1789

Science has many answers, but in the end, its high priests can only peel away at an infinite onion. There's impermanence to the scientific method; one never quite reaches solid bedrock. There's always a new observation, a new discovery, a radical theory, more testing to do. We look at the universe through a pinhole as God gradually reveals himself to us. The scientific method provides a road map as we zig and zag toward relative, temporary "truth." Science is a tool to help us observe, measure, and interpret the world — a *process* that helps us survive, adapt, and ultimately improve our lives. But there are no absolutes in a laboratory. "Science is always wrong. It never solves a problem without creating ten more," wrote George Bernard Shaw.

I (Paul) come to Christ through evidence and faith, but *with climate change no faith is required.* The evidence — what we can observe, test, and track — is compelling. And growing daily. But science is by no means a substitute for faith. Science has no answer for Absolute Truth. It has no clarity on *why we're here — and what comes next.* Science can't begin to describe the ultimate mystery of life and consciousness, the majesty of God's universe, or the promise of eternal life to come. A Babel of languages, quantum theories, and mathematical precision can't describe our God. Albert Einstein said, "Science without religion is lame, religion without science is blind." Science is essential — but fundamentally incomplete.

That doesn't mean we don't embrace the reality of today and see the world, not as we think it should be, but as it *really is* — the world we've influenced by releasing a trillion tons of carbon in the geological blink of an eye. Science is evidence-based. Look at the data. Test theories. Try to make sense of the world. To ignore science or question the integrity of scientists connecting the dots is to deny reality. When people ask me why more climate scientists don't debate professional skeptics in the media, I tell them the truth. At this point, it's the rough equivalent of debating gravity or the Apollo moon landings.

Do I *believe* in climate change? This isn't about belief or opinion. This is about acknowledging the data, taking time to understand the science, being mindful of what's happening worldwide, connecting dots, and making decisions based on the best available evidence. That's the thing about weather, science, and life: It never moves in a perfectly straight line. Science isn't a collection of immutable facts. *It's a process.* And right now some of the smartest minds on the planet are telling us to sit up and pay attention. As we have said, this isn't about polar bears. *This is about the health and welfare of our kids, and their kids, and their kids* . . . Respect for the unborn must extend to future generations of the unborn. Climate change is a global pro-life issue. Consistency matters. "Discounting future welfare or lives means weighting the welfare of lives of future people lower than lives now, irrespective of consumption and income levels, purely because their lives lie in the future," economist Nicholas Stern said. "This is discrimination by date of birth, and is unacceptable when viewed alongside notions of rights and justice."[1]

People of faith have good reason to be skeptical. "There is a general mistrust of scientists because they brought evolution and therefore a 'godless' origin," University of St. Thomas (Minnesota) climate scientist John Abraham tells me. "That mistrust was extended to climate change in many, but not all instances." There's something more at work here. If you don't accept the disease, you don't have to accept the cure, right? Abraham adds, "A major part of the reason climate science has become so ideological isn't about the science, it is about the proposed solutions. In many people's view, the solutions would be a burdensome and overreaching government intrusion into our lives and our liberties. Since we cannot have that, our minds force us to dismiss the science."[2]

My father fled communist East Germany and was fortunate to attend college at Wabash, in Indiana. He taught me many things, including to never take my freedom for granted. He is to this day a Reagan Republican—he embodies the very best conservative attributes. Growing up he taught me to take personal responsibility for my actions—that *all actions have consequences*. You can't dump sewage into a nearby lake or chemicals into a river, or pump hundreds of billions of tons of clear, odorless greenhouse gas into the atmosphere with impunity. There are consequences. But those costs, those "externalities," haven't been factored into a free market. Economist Nicholas Stern has called climate change the greatest and widest-ranging market failure ever seen, a failure to recognize the true costs of climate change, and price the external costs appropriately.[3] Clear, colorless, odorless exhaust gases from fossil fuels are vented directly into the atmosphere at a staggering rate, with no consequences. Out of sight, out of mind. We've privatized profits but spread the true costs of carbon pollution worldwide. And the price tag is now coming due.

I ask my conservative friends to keep an open mind—that this issue is very much about freedom. The freedom to live where you want to live, without fear of rising seas, perpetual drought, running out of water, or toxic weather hitting home every other month. The freedom to have any desired career. If you're a farmer, your job—already challenging—will become even more difficult in the future, as America's heartland flip-flops between tropical deluges and wilting heat and drought with greater frequency. "When I think of true conservatives, I think of people who take responsibility for their actions, pay their own way, and don't leave messes for others to clean up. They also care about being good stewards of God's creation. They are hard-headed realists who are strong enough to confront reality, even if it makes them uncomfortable," said Dr. Jonathan Koomey, Research Fellow at the Steyer-Taylor Center for Energy Policy and Finance at Stanford University.[4]

> What is a conservative after all but one who conserves, one who is committed to protecting and holding close the things by which we live. . . . And we want to protect and conserve the land on which we live—our countryside, our rivers and mountains, our plains and meadows and forests. This is our patrimony. This is what we leave

to our children. And our great moral responsibility is to leave it to them either as we found it or better than we found it.[5]

President Ronald Reagan

Conservatives conserve. I remember a time, not that long ago, when *conservative* and *conservation* went hand in hand, and there was deep respect for the scientific method. "There can be no greater issue than that of conservation in this country," said Teddy Roosevelt in 1912. Roosevelt kicked off America's National Park System, the envy of the world. Harry Truman launched the National Science Foundation. Richard Nixon launched the Environmental Protection Agency. Ronald Reagan consulted with scientists, supporting a ban on harmful chemicals eating away at the ozone layer. And George H. W. Bush signed the Clean Air Act into law and developed a market-based solution for acid rain. Amazingly, at one point there was almost unanimous, bipartisan support to protect the environment, to keep cleaning up our home. The votes for the 1970 Clean Air Act were 374 to 1 in the House and 73 to 0 in the Senate.[6] What changed? The balance between protecting our home and protecting the financial interests of campaign donors got seriously out of whack. When in doubt, follow the money.

It is difficult to get a man to understand something when his salary depends on his not understanding it.

Upton Sinclair

History shows a little manufactured misinformation can go a long way. The current strategy from special interests is similar to Big Tobacco congressional hearings held in the 1970s. *"You can't PROVE that smoking three packs a day of my client's product killed Aunt Betty!"* At the time we scratched our heads and those of us who smoked said, "Yes! The evidence simply isn't there." Today, is there anyone who seriously doubts that smoking increases the potential for lung cancer and heart disease? But tobacco companies trotted out a parade of (paid) scientists willing to cast doubt on sound science and delay a day of reckoning. Special interests and greed trumped the common good.

A nagging dependence on fossil fuels is killing us. That's not an exaggeration. Worldwide, an estimated 5.5 million people will die prematurely from breathing polluted air this year. In the United States, air pollution resulted in 79,000 premature deaths in 2013, more than twice as many as auto accidents.[7, 8]

> People will be lovers of themselves, lovers of money, boastful, proud, abusive, disobedient to their parents, ungrateful, unholy.
>
> 2 Timothy 3:2

This is tobacco—times a thousand. The amount of money in play with climate change runs into many trillions of dollars, and experts warn that most of the coal, oil, and gas will need to remain in the ground without risking dire, long-term consequences. Maybe God had the right idea burying carbon-based fuels deep underground. Staggering fossil fuel fortunes are on the line—and no industry wants to be disrupted. Fading industries have protected market share by questioning the science. Meanwhile, we're treating our collective home like a dirty ATM card. No harm, no foul. When

STATE COLLEGE, PENNSYLVANIA—Climate change is not a belief system, but a matter of evidence. The evidence comes from all aspects of our natural world: temperatures on land and in the ocean; melting ice and rising seas; and the responses by animals and plants. Civilization was built on a foundation of climate stability. Although we do not know exactly how the future will unfold, we cannot wait for 100 percent certainty to take action. In the military if you wait for 100 percent certainty, you will be 100 percent dead.

David W. Titley, Rear Admiral USN (retired); Director, Center for Solutions to Weather and Climate Risk, Penn State potential consequences get unpleasant, look away and change the subject. Better yet, question the so-called experts. The fossil fuel cartel is putting their short-term economic interests ahead of your interests and your kids' and grandkids' opportunity to live rich, full lives. Why? It's difficult to put a meter on the sun or the wind. Their business model depends on a captive audience lining up for their next fossil fuel fix—in perpetuity.

If you think the 2015 Syrian refugee crisis that engulfed Europe was traumatic, wait until widespread crop failures and water shortages force millions from their homes. Climate change impacts a wide range of fragile ecosystems, straining resources and igniting new conflicts.

A new level of climate volatility flavors and stresses global challenges and conflicts. Instead of salt, we're rubbing $CO2$ into the wounds. At least two-thirds of the global population, over 4 billion people, live with water scarcity for at least one month every year. Half a billion people live in places where water consumption is double the amount replenished by rain for the entire year, leaving them extremely vulnerable as underground aquifers run down, according to new research.[9] What happens when a nation runs out of water? That's why many within the U.S. military take the threat seriously.

The impacts of climate change may increase the frequency, scale, and complexity of future missions, including defense support to civil authorities, while at the same time undermining the capacity of our domestic installations to support training activities. Our actions to increase energy and water security, including investments in energy efficiency, new technologies, and renewable energy sources, will increase the resiliency of our installations and help mitigate these effects.[10]

U.S. Department of Defense

This comes down to risk management. We don't think twice about insuring our homes, our cars, and our health. But the planet, our atmosphere and oceans, the very thing that sustains us? *"Let's take a chance—what can go wrong?"* We are stewards. We all have a vested interest in treating God's creation with care and respect. This is about resolve, tenacity, and doing more than paying lip service to Scripture, because those who have the least will be first to be impacted by an erratic, noxious climate.

> The thief comes only to steal and kill and destroy; I have come that they may have life, and have it to the full.
>
> John 10:10

Katharine Hayhoe, a climate scientist and evangelical Christian at the Climate Science Center at Texas Tech University, said, "Christian values demand we take action. Climate change disproportionately affects the poor and vulnerable—the very people Christians are called to care for and love."[11]

Chances are your kids and grandkids get it. They aren't mocking the science or slandering scientists. They see what's happening. Will we sleepwalk into history, blaming political gridlock, fears of big government, and a need for cheap, dirty fuel to keep the lights on? Or will we rise to the occasion and find new ways to make markets less polluting and our way of life sustainable? Future generations will judge the actions we take today, because what worked in the 1940s probably won't work in the 2040s.

[God] is altogether glorious—unequalled in splendor and unrivaled in power. He is beyond the grasp of human reason—far beyond the grasp of any scientific mind. Inexhaustible, immeasurable, and unfathomable—eternal, immortal and invisible. The highest mountain peaks and the deepest canyon depths are just tiny echoes of His proclaimed greatness. And the blazing stars above, the faintest emblems of the full measure of His glory.[12]

Matt Redman

There is a place for both faith and science. "Science and faith work very well together," John Abraham explains. "Science tells us about the world as it is and will be. Faith informs our inquiries about why. Science keeps faith from superstition and faith helps make us human."

God is divine. His Son, Jesus, is divine. Would you say God's creation, our home, is divinely inspired and created? Yes? Then why on earth would we do anything to mess that up? It's important to keep an open mind, to respond to data and facts—both on the ground and in the air. One can have a deep faith in a Divine Creator and still respect scientists trying to make sense of our world—and our impact on God's creation. Actions have consequences. The signs are there. We should be mindful of what's happening *everywhere*.

I don't pretend to know the mind of God. No one can. But the Holy Bible tells us God made us in his self-image.[13] He gave us big, beautiful brains and the ability to think, reason, solve problems, make smart decisions, and improve our lives. And the good sense not to foul our nest.

Here's my long-range outlook, based on current weather and climate trends:

A major city will run out of water. Local officials will have no good options. A mega-fire will consume the suburbs of a large metropolitan area, fire fighters powerless to stop it. Only a reprieve in the weather will slow its advance. Not only Miami, but portions of Tampa, Norfolk, Annapolis, Boston, and the Bay Area will flood on sunny days, with a full moon exerting an additional tidal tug. The U.S. will see thousands of climate refugees permanently displaced from their homes. Extreme rains will flood a big city, disrupting life for hundreds of thousands of inhabitants for weeks. A large, violent EF-4 or EF-5 tornado will hit a downtown, with a loss of life rivaling Katrina in 2005. A Category-4 or 5 hurricane fueled by unusually warm water will devastate a major U.S. city with damage rising into the hundreds of billions of dollars. Drilling for fresh water will become more lucrative than fracking oil. Worldwide, more crops will fail and fresh-water shortages will increase over time. Residents of coastal Bangladesh will be forced inland by rising seas—a tidal wave of climate refugees igniting tensions with India. Wilting heat and perpetual drought around the Mediterranean Sea and Middle East will tempt millions to flee their homelands for northern Europe and Asia. Melting arctic ice will result in new shipping routes and arctic oil exploration, sparking new conflict with Russia. Government officials will wring their hands and point a finger of blame at each other, wondering why there was no warning, why contingency plans weren't put into place sooner. Americans will hold their representatives responsible for political paralysis and habitual climate inaction, demanding solutions.

Alarmist hype? Stay tuned.

CHAPTER 6

"Fear Not, for I Am With You"

Nor need we shrink from honestly facing conditions in our country today. This great Nation will endure as it has endured, will revive and will prosper. So, first of all, let me assert my firm belief that the only thing we have to fear is fear itself—nameless, unreasoning, unjustified terror which paralyzes needed efforts to convert retreat into advance.

Franklin D. Roosevelt (1933)

A little fear goes a long way, according to the old saying. Unfortunately, there is too much fear spread around when it comes to discussing climate change and making meaningful decisions to address what Paul and I call the greatest moral challenge of our time. This moment should be our greatest opportunity to build a new-energy economy. While a shrinking few still try to deny the scientific reality of climate change, Americans and people overseas daily face the impacts of our warming world. Ironically, those being the most tragically harmed now are the world's poorest populations who have contributed the least to greenhouse gas pollution. We need to care for the least of these, as the Bible commands us, and stop fearing fear itself.

It reminds me of being a first-time parent. Having a child is scary; our unknown role with the first causes most of us to go overboard. I remember making sure every item in the house was clean and sterilized. God forbid if a pacifier hit the floor and wasn't washed in boiling water, or if our child wasn't rushed to the pediatrician at the first sign of a runny nose, or the grandparents didn't go to the latest parenting classes. However, by the second child, eating the dog's food doesn't result in an emergency room visit, and that thrown-on-the-floor "binky" gets wiped off on the baby blanket or thoroughly cleaned by a quick insertion into Dad or Mom's mouth.

That's not to say we ignore safety or health risks. We just put it into perspective. We still use the least harmful cleaning products, ensure the storage cabinet has locks, and get the recommended vaccinations. We don't allow our grandchildren to play in the street or even go unsupervised to the playground, and we use organic fertilizer on our gardens. Simply put, we've learned to understand and then address the risks.

Fear has been used way too often by environmental groups and deniers alike. Many remember the Heartland Institute's billboards depicting climate believers as Osama bin Laden, and some environmental groups proclaiming the Keystone XL pipeline's construction would be the end of the world. This is not to say that the production and development of Alberta's tar sands are a good creation care practice, but to be "game over" for climate change, the tar sands development would have to increase almost exponentially from its current production. With the current oil price, the unconventional drilling advances in the United States, and Middle East production, the economics simply aren't there. By a similar token, Paul and I are evangelical Christians and lifelong Republicans, not terrorists, and certainly do not believe in grand conspiracy theories. We understand the realities of climate change, their current related health impacts, and the folly it would be to ignore conservative moral and economic values regarding our nation's future.

Jim Ball has been leading the charge in defense of God's creation for almost two decades. When I first became leader of the Evangelical Environmental Network (EEN), he pulled me aside and said, "We don't need to make climate change any worse, it's already bad enough." Jim's right, and one of his current tasks at EEN is to ensure we don't make any over-the-top claims. Both EEN's ministry and this book desire to provide a moral message that offers realistic assessments of how humanity's use of fossil fuels is already changing the creation around us and harming our kids. We're searching for a way to overcome climate change in harmony with our conservative values to create a better America.

Social science research is clear: Fear doesn't drive people to accept the reality of climate change.[1] As an example, hurricanes and tornadoes are not caused by our changing climate, but climate change does provide the energy to make them worse. It's weather on steroids. Not every bad storm is climate-related, as some have attempted to claim, but many storms are.

Hurricane Sandy, nicknamed Superstorm Sandy because it was so massive, is a good case in point. The media talked ad nauseam about the climate/superstorm connection. Still, despite New Jersey's masterful slogan "Stronger Than the Storm" and the media hype, Sandy still didn't move the national needle for addressing climate change. Human resiliency overcame and discounted the increased climate impacts, at least in most American minds.

Fear has worked well for those who wish for inaction and keeping the status quo on fossil fuel uses. It's much easier to tap into our basic fear of change, big government, and taking money from our pockets. Our role as evangelicals requires us to overcome our fears and the amplification of them by those wishing to ignore the realities for their benefit. Fear comes from trusting in ourselves instead of placing trust in the Creator. Some out in cyberspace have posted that *fear not* appears 365 times in the Bible, once for each day of the year. The reality is that *fear not* or some variation appears around a hundred times. Regardless, the frequency reflects our propensity to fear. And sadly, fear often gets in the way of hoping for a better life.

Most people know the beginning of the Exodus narrative, thanks to Hollywood, Charlton Heston, and the more recent film *Exodus* with Christian Bale. Fewer people, however, know "the rest of the story."

Moses, through God, leads the Israelite refugees through Sinai to the edge of the Promised Land. He then sends twelve men, one from each tribe, to explore the "land of milk and honey." After forty days they return, filled with outstanding opportunities of hope. And some challenges. Two men, Caleb and Joshua, see the opportunity and understand the hope for a better future. They cry out before Israel, "Do not be afraid." The other ten, overcome with fear, forget what God has already accomplished. The Lord brought these sojourners through multiple trials, yet through fear, the ten fermented yet another revolt against God and Moses, crying out, "If only we had died in Egypt."

Returning to Egypt was an oft-repeated fear throughout the Exodus wanderings. And for many today, it's much easier to accept the past than see the hope in a new future. As a pastor, I led a congregation through transition from a "caring for its members" church to a mission-driven church. The fear of change, growth, and biblical understanding made me the subject of many parking lot discussions, phone calls, and sadly, people leaving. One of the most telling stories happened as we tried to teach biblical stewardship.

We had been building toward a commitment Sunday with a series of worship themes designed around stewardship. On the Sunday before the "big day," I preached on tithing. Immediately following worship, one of our elders stormed into my study, threw his church keys on my desk, and said, "How dare you talk about money today. That was supposed to be next week, and I wasn't going to come." He stormed out and never returned. Instead of biblical inspiration, this gentleman allowed his fear and "his" money to support his past and not consider new paradigms.

Whether it's money, creation care, or a host of other subjects, we don't like change. Change forces us to transform, think differently, and in some cases admit that our actions weren't the best. One of my favorite tongue-in-cheek sayings, "I thought I made a mistake once, but I was wrong," conveys much of our own internal reasoning. It's no different when it comes to climate change and energy. Many want us to continue living in the past; there are many loud voices that want us to go back to Egypt.

In evangelical circles, the first attempt usually centers on a misused Scripture passage. One of the most cited passages is Genesis 8:22:

> As long as the earth endures, seedtime and harvest,
> cold and heat, summer and winter,
> day and night will never cease.

No climate expert has ever decreed that the earth won't endure or that seasons will cease. But our seasons are changing, as we're seeing all over the world. My south central Pennsylvania home now has the climate Richmond, Virginia, did approximately twenty years ago. Earlier in this book we shared the changing rainfall patterns in Malawi. The oceans have warmed, glaciers are melting, and sea level is rising.

What the folks who quote the above and similar Scriptures are saying is that God is in control and nothing happens without God's command. This sovereignty of God theology, when taken to the utmost, believes that nothing happens without God's permission. While I affirm God is in ultimate control, this ultra-orthodox Calvinist

It's not about saving the planet. . . . It's about helping people, real people who are being affected by climate change today. Higher energy bills for air conditioning. Freak rainstorms and droughts wiping out their food supply. Rising sea level threatening their homes and fields. It's the poor and disadvantaged who are being hardest hit: those very people the Bible tells us to care for.[2]

Dr. Katharine Hayhoe

position doesn't match John Calvin's views on creation care, nor does it allow free will and the consequences of sin to be human choices.

Once, as I was giving a climate presentation, an Iowa farmer started asking me question after question about God's control. After several back and forths, I asked, "Do you believe God causes earthquakes?" After a few moments, the man replied, "I guess I do." I then went on to say that we have a different understanding of God, and we'll just have to agree to disagree. I respectfully moved on. After all the questions and discussion, a colleague attempted to reach out to the farmer. Upon approaching my questioner, my associate saw the man surrounded by his friends and neighbors. From the circle, directed to my disagreeing friend, my associate overheard, "Hey, Joe, the next time one of your hogs get sick, you're not going to waste money calling the vet, are you?"

It's very interesting when our professed theology meets our real life. And in "real life," our climate *is* changing. As mentioned in the introduction, my ninety-year-old dad, a former coal miner, made the connection just by looking at the world outside his window. My prayer is that you will be encouraged to spend time with God in creation. Simply observe the seasons in your neighborhood. In the continental United States, for example, autumn leaves are lasting an average of ten days longer and spring is starting about four days earlier.[3] Birdwatchers tell us birds are nesting farther north than ever before, and planting season has significantly changed.

Get connected to the wondrous creation and see for yourself what we are doing to our beautiful common home.

Our eyes don't see what they don't wish to see; our chief blindness is change. Moving forward is hard. Even with hundreds of years of slavery, abuse, and ridicule, the Israelites cried out at least twelve separate times to return to Egypt. Seemingly every time they encountered an obstacle they wanted to return to the past. Slavery and almost certain death appeared more palatable than following God's lead into a new future.

Thankfully, the early pioneers of our nation didn't succumb to the same anxiety. Leaders like William Bradford, Roger Williams, and especially independence champions such as George Washington and Thomas Jefferson faced certain death if they retreated to the past. We won't face the gallows from climate change, but our children will continue suffering, our military will increasingly be put in harm's way, millions around the world will die, and the world's economy will suffer. It's well past time to plant our standard

The reason I am so focused on solar now is because I believe that solar empowers the people. I believe that solar equals energy freedom. The average person cannot go out and construct a new power plant, they can't put a nuclear reactor on their rooftop, they can't go out and build a big windfarm. But they can install solar panels on their rooftop and become energy independent. Also, during my research I found out that there is nothing more centralized in our nation nor at risk of a terrorist attack than our power grid. The National Energy Regulatory Commission found that a terrorist would just have to take down nine key substations out of more than 54,000 and it would cause a blackout from coast to coast. So that made it even more important and even more vital for me to push for decentralized energy and, in particular, solar.[4]

Debbie Dooley, founding member of the Tea Party movement

and go toward a "promised land" of energy freedom, energy independence, the liberty for healthy unpolluted lives, and the right to build a solid economy.

Retreat is no longer an option. All across America energy freedom is springing up on household rooftops. But opponents of energy freedom have been attempting to hold back the future. Many utility monopolies are pushing hard to limit energy freedom, using their influence to restrict home solar installations or set exorbitant net metering fees on home solar panels without considering the benefits, and the guise they're using is customer protection.

That's what David Owens, a senior official for the trade association for stockholder-owned electric utilities, said about efforts to thwart individuals from being able to produce their own clean electricity via rooftop solar panels. "It's not about profits; it's about protecting customers," said Owens.[5]

It's difficult to accept those words at face value. Since their beginning, the coal and utility industries' reputation as good neighbors has lacked. I know firsthand real stories of company towns, poor working conditions, and maximizing profits at the sake of others. While businesses like Dow Chemical, M&M Mars, and even Walmart spend billions for energy efficiency, big coal spends as little as possible in research and pollution control. Only when forced by regulations did the coal industry address mine safety, black lung disease, acid rain, mercury pollution, and all forms of water pollution and land reclamation. Even today, the scars of coal mining mar creation's beauty.

My dad's favorite deer hunting location rests on the side of a Pennsylvania mountain whose top was removed by strip mining. The land was never reclaimed—it continues spewing acid mine drainage into the remaining forest. The washout, as it's called, grows each year—destroying trees and habitats, and eventually the toxic runoff disappears into the water table. As a child and teenager, I thought this was just the cost of electricity and jobs—what a mistake!

Some continue to falsely claim that coal produces the cheapest electricity, but at least one study states that when you factor in all the external costs from coal, including medical bills, lost lives, and property damage, coal electricity is triple what you pay at the meter.[6] It may appear cheap, but each of us pays the price in our children's health, insurance premiums, and polluted water and air. Confirming that coal isn't cheap and is dying as an electric-generating fuel, Appalachian Power President Charles Patton said recently, "You just can't go with new coal [plants] at this point in time. . . . It is just not economically feasible to do so."[7] By 2026, Appalachian Power expects its use of coal power to be down 26 percent. One leading utility, Xcel Energy, which serves mainly in the Midwest, is transitioning from coal energy to renewables and has announced a goal to reduce its carbon emissions by 60 percent by the year 2030.[8]

History teaches us that those who seize opportunities come out better on the other side. Mark Zuckerberg, Bill Gates, Steve Jobs, and Elon Musk are just a few in our current day, but few remember some of the many ill-fated business decisions made in the desire to keep the status quo. Western Union declined to purchase the telephone from Alexander Graham Bell, as they considered it just an electronic toy. Our defense industry considered the Wright brothers a joke, and Kodak executives, who patented the digital camera in 1977, thought it unwise to market it.

We stand today on the precipice of a new future with amazing hope for new opportunities, yet some would want us to continue living in a past that is doomed to failure and literally death to many of God's children. Those with vested interests want to continue the status quo, or at least delay the future for as long as possible. Living in the past offers no opportunity for a future blessed with pure air, clean water, and an economy filled with new jobs. As a father, I had one overarching lesson for my kids: You can't change the past, but you can determine the future. We all make mistakes, and all of us at some point would have liked to change at least part of the past, but we can't. So let's take on the future, and with God's help take on the challenges.

We've faced similar opportunities before. As Wall Street columnist Michael Silverstein wrote a few years ago, many questioned the practicality of changing to the automobile from the horse. There were no roads, no gas stations, and horses were the third-largest industry in the United States at the end of the nineteenth century, only surpassed by railroads and farming.[9] There were many who fought the change, and yet the automobile now drives America.

For the past few hundred years we have relied on fossil fuels as our primary energy source. First it was wood, then coal, and for the past century oil and natural gas. There is no doubt about the economic benefit fossil fuels brought to our economy. Energy remains the absolute key to development in any society, and especially to the two billion people around the world with limited or no access to electricity. We, in the developed world, have benefited greatly from our past energy sources, but only in the past fifty years have we begun to understand the costs borne by our energy choices. These costs are mounting.

Insurance claims, material shortages, and lost productivity are just a few of the economic threats associated with our changing climate. A few business giants like Bloomberg, Apple, Nike, Mars, and others have acknowledged climate change and been part of the solution for quite some time. Some might remember when Nike, Apple, and even Pacific Gas and Electric quit the U.S. Chamber of Commerce back in 2009 over the Chamber's radical denial stance. But not until recently have economists and greater numbers of businesses joined in the efforts to address climate change. In 2015, General Mills, one of the largest food corporations, announced new commitments to lower its carbon footprint. "We recognize that we must do our part to protect and conserve natural resources. Our business depends on it and so does the planet," stated Ken Powell, chairman and CEO of General Mills.[10] Months later, Unilever, Kellogg, and seven other corporations joined General Mills in an open letter to U.S. congressional leaders:

> The challenge presented by climate change will require all of us—government, civil society and business—to do more with less. For companies like ours, that means producing more food on less land using fewer natural resources. If we don't take action now, we risk not only today's livelihoods but also those of future generations.[11]

They're not alone; ten of the world's largest energy companies—including BP, Royal Dutch Shell, and Total—recently announced their shared ambition to limit the rise of global average temperature 2 degrees Celsius, which is the maximum manageable increase before catastrophic impacts: "[We] support the implementation of clear stable policy frameworks consistent with a 2°C future; these will help our companies to take informed decisions and make effective and sustainable contributions to addressing climate change."[12] Noticeably missing from this statement were big American energy firms ExxonMobil and Chevron. In fairness, though, they both recognize the reality of climate change, and ExxonMobil supports a revenue neutral carbon fee as a policy approach.[13] And in what is

A Call to Action

We lament over the widespread abuse and destruction of the earth's resources, including its bio-diversity. Probably the most serious and urgent challenge faced by the physical world now is the threat of climate change. This will disproportionately affect those in poorer countries, for it is there that climate extremes will be most severe and where there is little capability to adapt to them. World poverty and climate change need to be addressed together and with equal urgency.[15]

National Association of Evangelicals (2015)

seemingly a change in corporate direction, ExxonMobil recently issued the following:

> We recognize that our past participation in broad coalitions that opposed ineffective climate policies subjects us to criticism by climate activist groups. We will continue to advocate for policies that reduce emissions while enabling economic growth.[14]

This shift mirrors the American public as well. A University of Texas poll indicated 75 percent of all Americans accept the scientific reality of climate change, with 59 percent of Republicans saying climate change is occurring, up ten percentage points from six months earlier.[16] There are probably numerous factors for this large uptick in conservatives who accept the reality of climate change, but based on my travels across the United States, it's a combination of the massive increase in renewable energy (and its lower cost), the severe weather—especially the western drought —and the faith/moral message championed by Pope Francis and then affirmed by the National Association of Evangelicals' call to action. These forces, working together or separately, have spurred folks to reevaluate options and look beyond the rhetoric to the reality.

Several years ago at a Q Conference (the evangelical version of TED Talks) in Washington D.C., I was asked about the reality of climate change. My response: Don't believe me without researching the facts for yourself. Don't listen to twenty-second sound bites on Fox News or MSNBC or talk radio. Take the time to examine the facts for yourself. See what our National Academy of Science publishes, study the issues from different perspectives, look what Christians around the world are saying. Who has what at risk? Who are the business "winners" and "losers"?

In conversations after the talk and in emails after the meeting, I received lots of comments about appreciating the advice. It seemed to empower people to look past talking heads and engage their minds, and I invite you to do the same. Take time to read the

Scriptures, use some of the resources recommended in this book, and go beyond to examine credible nonbiased scientific organizations and faith groups.

One thing of which I am truly convinced is that special interests, both liberal and conservative, have tilted government policies in

---

Risky Business

The American economy is already beginning to feel the effects of climate change. These impacts will likely grow materially over the next five to twenty-five years and affect the future performance of today's business and investment decisions in the following areas:

Coastal property and infrastructure. Within the next fifteen years, higher sea levels combined with storm surge will likely increase the average annual cost of coastal storms along the Eastern Seaboard and the Gulf of Mexico by $2 billion to $3.5 billion. Adding in potential changes in hurricane activity, the likely increase in average annual losses grows to up to $7.3 billion, bringing the total annual price tag for hurricanes and other coastal storms to $35 billion.

Agriculture. A defining characteristic of agriculture in the U.S. is its ability to adapt. But the adaptation challenge going forward for certain farmers in specific counties in the Midwest and South will be significant. Without adaptation, some Midwestern and Southern counties could see a decline in yields of more than 10 percent over the next five to twenty-five years should they continue to sow corn, wheat, soy, and cotton, with a one-in-twenty chance of yield losses of these crops of more than 20 percent.

Energy. Greenhouse gas-driven changes in temperature will likely necessitate the construction of up to 95 gigawatts of new power generation capacity over the next five to twenty-five years—the equivalent of roughly two hundred average coal or natural gas-fired power plants—costing residential and commercial ratepayers up to $12 billion per year.[17]

---

favor of different industries at different times and thus have hindered any semblance of a market economy. However, before going down the rabbit hole of subsidies, let's return to the business world at hand.

One way to examine climate change uses risk analysis, such as the data presented in the sidebar story "Risky Business," published by a group led by former New York Mayor Michael Bloomberg. Additional research from Sanford University predicts the global economy will contract by 23 percent if climate change goes unchecked.[18] Although important and informing, risk avoidance is too much like fear. Since calculated risk analysis is a future event, it's easier to dismiss as we focus on the present. We tell ourselves that there are enough problems for today, and some evangelicals might even quote Jesus: "Therefore do not worry about tomorrow, for tomorrow will worry about itself. Each day has enough trouble of its own."[19]

If you are a recent college graduate working in fast food, with $50,000 in college loans, or a former thirty-dollar-per-hour skilled manufacturing employee now forced into three separate part-time jobs to pay your mortgage, climate change is far too distant to be relevant. It's the same in rural towns or urban areas. Where once we had manufacturing jobs, now we have either no employment or under-employment. Lee Iacocca commented in his 1984 autobiography that the skilled, high-paid worker was key to America's middle class and economy.[20] Based on current economic conditions, it's hard to disagree with him. However, we're not going back to the future. Many of the old high-end manufacturing jobs are gone for good. It's no use complaining or even discussing the pros and cons about NAFTA (North American Free Trade Agreement) or other potential trade pacts. It's time to move forward and create a new well-paid labor market; one that's already emerging is renewable energy.

One in eighty new jobs in the United States since the financial crisis comes from renewable energy,[21] and solar already employs

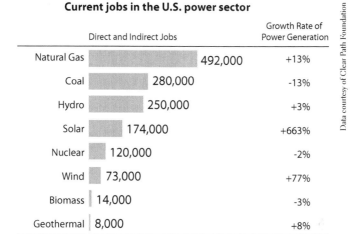

Current jobs in the U.S. power sector

	Direct and Indirect Jobs	Growth Rate of Power Generation
Natural Gas	492,000	+13%
Coal	280,000	-13%
Hydro	250,000	+3%
Solar	174,000	+663%
Nuclear	120,000	-2%
Wind	73,000	+77%
Biomass	14,000	-3%
Geothermal	8,000	+8%

Data courtesy of Clear Path Foundation

approximately twice as many folks as coal mining. From 2008 to 2012, the coal industry lost 49,000 jobs, and renewable energy plus natural gas gained four times as many.[22]

It's not just increased jobs; the energy market is changing as well. Just look at Tesla and its behemoth battery plant being built in Nevada. The company's investment, jobs, and products are game changers. History may record the moment this so-called Gigafactory starts production as more transformative to our economy and technological future than President Kennedy's announcement to put a human on the moon.

On a smaller scale, one of my favorite success stories is Pennsylvania's Brookville Equipment Corporation. Making the transition away from being a coal equipment supplier, they recently earned an innovation award for their Liberty Modern Streetcar featuring an onboard energy storage system. The award recognizes new technology in a wireless streetcar design being implemented in Dallas, Detroit, and Washington, D.C. Companies like Brookville aren't looking backward but recognizing their strengths—they're moving forward.

Tesla's mission is to accelerate the world's transition to sustainable transportation. To achieve that goal, we must produce electric vehicles in sufficient volume to force change in the automobile industry. With a planned production rate of 500,000 cars per year in the latter half of this decade, Tesla alone will require today's entire worldwide production of lithium ion batteries. The Tesla Gigafactory was born of necessity and will supply enough batteries to support our projected vehicle demand.

Tesla broke ground on the Gigafactory in June 2014 outside Sparks, Nevada, and we expect to begin cell production in 2017. By 2020, the Gigafactory will reach full capacity and produce more lithium ion batteries annually than were produced worldwide in 2013. . . .

We expect to drive down the per kilowatt hour (kWh) cost of our battery pack by more than 30 percent. The Gigafactory will also be powered by renewable energy sources, with the goal of achieving net zero energy.[23]

Tesla Motors

This isn't some illusion or pipedream. Business giant Bloomberg New Energy Finance says the clean energy *transition* is now self-sustaining and inevitable.[24] Morgan Stanley, another business giant, says the "tipping point is near for going off the grid."[25] In what is great news for the consumer and the planet alike, NV Energy entered into an agreement with First Solar for 100 megawatts of electricity at 3.87 cents a kilowatt-hour. That's almost 10 cents per kilowatt cheaper than NV Energy paid for renewable electricity just the year before.[26] Solar costs have declined dramatically, with the price of photovoltaic panels declining over 70 percent since 2010 and overall system costs dropping by 9 percent for residential and 21 percent for utility-sized systems from 2013 to 2014. According to the same report, the price decline continues as incentives and subsidies are disappearing.[27]

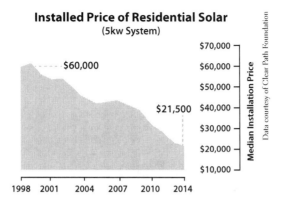

As market-based fiscal conservatives, Paul and I believe it's past time for governments to get out of the energy subsidy business. Energy subsidies have been a constant corporate handout seemingly forever in the United States, and it's almost impossible to calculate the amount of these subsidies for any of the fossil fuels. It's clear that at a minimum, our federal government provides $4.9 billion each year to fossil fuels. Additional estimates stretch as high as $18.5 billion per year, according to the progressive advocacy organization Oil Change International. Others argue that if you include military costs in the Middle East, for example, the price could soar beyond $60 billion per year. Although older, a report funded by the nuclear industry states that U.S. subsidies totaled $584 billion dollars for fossil fuels (70 percent) and $74 billion for renewables (9 percent) from 1950 to 2010.[28]

Special interests have always promoted fossil fuels with policy makers and in the American public heart. As President George W. Bush once said, "We have a serious problem: America is addicted to oil." Through almost a hundred years of hidden costs and government benefits, these dead fuels enabled a false market and guided an unsustainable American way of life. Instead of developing better public transit, we built superhighways. Cheap gas built suburbia and continues to fuel a self-actualization of independence instead of

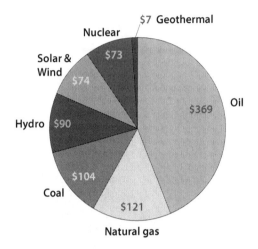

U.S. federal energy subsidies (1950–2010)
Billions in 2010 dollars

shared responsibility in community. Even with the oil embargo of the late 1970s and early '80s and the greater reliance on foreign oil, we grew more addicted instead of seeking alternatives.

A national energy policy (that we don't have) and knowing true costs would have inspired American entrepreneurship long ago, instead of beginning just now. How many Elon Musks did we lose just because our government picked the "energy winner" long ago?

Some readers may be quick to jump to a false conclusion or perhaps call foul because we haven't mentioned renewable subsidies yet. From 2009 to 2014, the U.S. government provided approximately $10 billion each year to renewable energy.[29] That $50 billion or so is roughly $20 billion more than fossil fuels over the same period. However, according to *Forbes*, from 1994 to 2009, fossil benefited with approximately $447 billion in subsidies compared to $6 billion for renewables. So in roughly the last twenty years the score is dead fuel—$477 billion; living fuel—$56 billion. And the score doesn't include the tax breaks that started in 1916 for fossil fuels. Moreover, the highly respected International Energy Agency (IEA) reported that fossil fuels are securing $550 billion a year in subsidies worldwide and holding back investment in cleaner forms of energy. Oil, coal, and gas received more than four times the $120 billion paid out in incentives for renewables, including wind, solar, and biofuels.[30]

The simple answer: Remove all energy subsidies. Some will say that's unfair to renewables since fossil has received subsidies for what seems like forever. Fossil fuel interests will cry foul, that it's another war on our industry. Others will say that if the rest of the world is doing it, we can't stop. But somehow, someone must choose morality and act with fairness. It will require major political will, as the only way to ensure vacating all the subsidies is to revise our tax code, and quite honestly, the only way to accomplish this miracle is for us to express our ethical values and hold elected

Solar Power Changes Lives

Deep in northern Kenya, above Napuu Village, there is only the brightest of full moons to light the way. You can hear the chatter as villagers sit around open fires, but with the nearest power station more than 200km (124 miles) away, there is nothing else to light up the village. Here, power is a precious thing and only a few can enjoy what many take for granted.

But inside David Lodio's small home—two rooms made of [cinder] blocks and mud—there is light. His family watches television, his six children do their homework without candles. There is no need for expensive kerosene lamps—all because of a single solar panel on his tin roof. "When we started using the solar panels, life changed in a good way," says Mr. Lodio. . . . "The children could do their homework well, the children could watch the news and football on TV. I am seeing my children reading and writing well," he explains.[32]

officials accountable until change happens. We have the political power to do just that.

In the 2014 midterm elections, evangelical Christians represented 26 percent of actual voters. Seventy percent of evangelicals voted Republican in both the 2014 midterms and the 2012 presidential elections. In the same 2014 midterms, white Catholics represented 19 percent of the votes cast, and 60 percent of those voted Republican as well. So the conservative faith community represents almost 50 percent of America. If we unite, we will put us on the road to overcoming climate change, defending our kids and offering them a future.

Let's work together and force a framework to correct for true costs (correcting market failures) and then end all subsidies. In several states, renewables are at or near parity with fossil fuels without counting the hidden costs.[31] By adding the costs, we can rebuild America with a clean energy future based on market and conservative values instead of government regulations.

The good news is that renewables are beginning to win on their own, both in the United States and around the world. They need to, out of necessity. About 1.2 billion people have no access to electricity, another 2 billion have only limited electric availability, and approximately 2.6 billion people still use traditional cooking methods, causing 1.5 million deaths per year from indoor air pollution. As mentioned earlier, energy is key to development and essential for the rest of the world. A few, clinging to the past, have attempted to cry out that climate change action would continue and even exacerbate the lack of modern energy, known as energy poverty. They promote coal-fired utilities as the only way to overcome this energy blight.

It's time to turn energy poverty into energy prosperity. And market-based solutions, including entrepreneurship, are providing the foothold. One example is M-Kopa Solar, which operates in Kenya, Uganda, and Tanzania. Named by *Forbes* as one of the top fifty companies changing the world, M-Kopa Solar now provides solar power to over 250,000 previously off-grid homes, adding five hundred more each day.[33]

Their business model takes advantage of current conditions. In many African locales, families spend between 45 and 60 cents per day on kerosene or other dirty fuels. This represents 20 to 30 percent of their daily income. For a small down payment, M-Kopa installs a solar system and collects the daily fee, usually equal to or below what the family paid for kerosene or on cell phones or other mobile devices. After a year, a family can upgrade its system based on family need and successful payment history. As has happened with cell phones leap-frogging landlines in much of the world, "distributed" electricity, which uses no central generating system, is vaulting over the past.

M-Kopa Solar and others are taking advantage of an existing market and improving the quality of life. The existing fuels market is estimated at $10 billion per year in Africa, and these energy entrepreneurs provide a cleaner, healthier, and lower-cost alternative while making a profit.

> Investing in off-grid and mini-grid renewables, as solar costs fall and battery technology improves, [are] by far the most cost-effective solutions. Coal is therefore not the cheapest or most appropriate option for many of those without access to energy as its proponents claim. If the costs and inefficiencies of carbon capture and storage (CCS) are also added, then this just makes coal even less competitive. CCS will hopefully have a role in the future, but even optimistic . . . scenarios do not see widespread deployment until post-2030. Making those without energy access in regions that have coal resources wait another couple of decades is not the urgent solution they need.[34]
>
> Anthony Hobley, Chief Executive
> of the Carbon Tracker Initiative

Companies like M-Kopa aren't isolated cases. The majority world is deploying renewables over old-fashioned fossil-fuel power. Solar installations are doubling every two years, with developing countries installing renewable energy projects at nearly double the rate of developed nations. In fact, global emissions of carbon dioxide flatlined in 2014, while the global economy grew that same year. It was the first time in forty years that we experienced a halt or reduction in carbon dioxide emissions without an economic downturn, according to the International Energy Agency.

This doesn't mean no new coal-fired plants will be built. There are over two thousand coal-based electric-generating stations planned worldwide, and if even 30 percent are built, it will be difficult to meet the 2-degree Celsius target that most experts say will limit the worst climate change impacts. However, numerous market conditions suggest many of the coal plants won't be built. First, as discussed, renewable energy prices are falling. Second, the capital cost for renewables is considerably lower. Third, renewable deployment is easier and faster, and last, the health costs, not including climate change, are forcing coal plant closings. While there is not universal agreement on the final outcome, our anticipated winner is renewable energy.

According to the international financial giant McKinsey and Company, the total projected investment to electrify sub-Saharan Africa by 2040 is $490 billion for new generating capacity, plus another $345 billion for transmission and distribution.[35] The needed capital for both generation and transmission is massive and will require international aid.

Because most financial institutions view fossil fuels as a poor investment, the funds to build these two thousand coal plants are drying up. The World Bank, numerous European nations, and the United States are limiting capital for coal and other fossil fuels. All of them are agreeing with us that the real cost of coal-generated electricity already exceeds other generation methods. With Xcel

Energy and other American utilities making the same financial choice, it's hard to consider the majority world arriving at a different conclusion.

Practically any time you mention climate change or clean energy, China is part of the discussion. The rhetoric is high about clean energy hurting our economy while China does nothing about climate change. It seems that we're afraid of China, but the real truth is that China is afraid of itself. China has installed more coal-fired electric generation stations than any other nation in the past thirty years and has developed quicker than any other country.

You might recall the Beijing Olympics. The Chinese stopped automobile traffic and closed power plants to defuse the air pollution and falsify world perceptions during the games. However, the Chinese modernization, including increased electric capacity without environmental controls, is literally killing its people. Every day an average of four thousand people die from air pollution, an amazing 1.6 million per year.[36] The same coal that provides electric power is generating massive amounts of smog. At the same time, 20 percent of its farmland is polluted,[37] and the Chinese state newspaper has admitted almost 60 percent of the water is unfit to drink.[38] In addition, one study found that 66 percent of Chinese wealthy were thinking of leaving China.[39] Pollution is destabilizing the Chinese populace, and China won't permit internal turmoil.

China has already taken serious action in reducing pollution. In 2014, they adopted new environmental protection laws, limited transportation, shuttered some coal-fired generating stations, and continued as the world's number one producer and user of renewable energy. They invested $83 billion in renewables and deployed over 13 gigawatts of solar and 20.8 wind-generated gigawatts, while the U.S. installed almost 10 gigawatts of solar and wind. As a comparison, the 33.8 gigawatts of renewables installed in one year equals 3.5 percent of the United States' total electric capacity. By 2020, China expects to have installed over 350 gigawatts of wind and solar, or roughly one-third of our capacity. China knows renewables and is leading the world in their installations and supplying clean energy to the world.

So when asked if China (and for that matter, India) is serious about its public commitments to a healthier climate, the answer is yes. The commitments are not enough—only a beginning—but if the Chinese want to avoid national destabilization, they must act.

Worldwide, we face many challenges, but American ingenuity combined with declining renewable energy costs can allay our fears. More important, we have a fearless God who empowers us to take these challenges head on. Will we wander in the wilderness and fail to take on the challenges, or make the American dream happen again? Many people consider the next twenty years as the greatest opportunity for prosperity of all time.

The choice is ours. Today we stand on the precipice of a new-energy "promised land." Within our grasp is a clean energy revolution. A revolution that could provide energy freedom for all, add to our economy, save our children's health, bring billions into the twenty-first-century world, and reduce security threats to our nation. Ben Franklin is attributed as once saying, "Doing well by doing good." It's time to live this biblically inspired saying.

Evangelicals, other people of faith, and all people of good must lead in creating a clean energy economy—it's who God calls us to be. Within our grasp is clean air, pure water, healthier children, and well-paying jobs,[40] all combining into a brighter American economy. We will have the power to choose energy freedom and assist in literally transforming the lives of billions around the world with energy prosperity. The clean energy transition is already under way and unstoppable; however, the revolution depends on our grabbing the opportunity and Caleb and Joshua's hope. We can choose fear and continue living in the past—retreating back to "Egypt," simply wandering in the wilderness, and waiting for this generation to disappear. Or we can choose life by seizing the hope and investing in a new, clean-energy future.

CHAPTER 7

Silver Buckshot

You can always count on Americans to do the right thing—after they've tried everything else.

Winston Churchill

I'm proud of having been one of the first to recognize that states and the federal government have a duty to protect our natural resources from the damaging effects of pollution that can accompany industrial development.

Ronald Reagan

Man has been appointed as a steward for the management of God's property, and ultimately he will give account for his stewardship.

Paraphrase of Luke 16:2

Climate change is the "perfect" problem. It's global, we're all contributing to the rapid rise of warming gases, and there's no simple way out. Psychologists tell us we're all innately wired to ignore, delay, or deny a problem with no obvious solution. "Climate change is a problem that politics is almost designed not to solve. Its costs lie mostly in the distant future, whereas politics is built to respond to immediate conditions," says commentator Jonathan Chait. "There has not yet been a galvanizing Pearl Harbor moment, when the urgency of action becomes instantly clear and isolationists melt away. Instead, it breeds counterproductive mental reactions: denial, fatalism, and depression."[1]

Relying on dirty fossil fuels in perpetuity represents a fundamental injustice. Putting the profits of corporate polluters ahead of the health of today's children—and the welfare of future generations—is a dark, Darwinian experiment; immoral and ultimately unsustainable. Can we gradually dial down dirty fossil fuels and ramp up a new, clean-energy economy? Yes. At some point pragmatism and common sense will prevail. In fact, it's already happening.

There may be no silver bullet yet. But there's plenty of *silver buckshot*—hundreds of new technologies and viable, cost-competitive clean energy alternatives, which will gradually, methodically wean us off fossil fuels, employ more Americans, and jump-start a sputtering, rudderless economy.

Why are Mitch and I optimistic? Because of the ingenuity and tenacity of America's entrepreneurs. And Moore's Law.

Moore's Law relates to the dramatic and continuing reduction in the size and cost of computer technology. But it also applies to photovoltaic devices (solar panels), where costs dropped an astonishing 75 percent between 2009 and 2014, about 10 percent each year. America's clean energy sector grew by 14 percent in 2014, roughly five times as much as the rest of the economy.[2] God had the wisdom to give us a reliable, safe, and free energy source: a massive fusion reactor 93 million miles overhead. As CNN's Fareed Zakaria reported recently, "Every six hours, more solar energy reaches the world's deserts than all of humanity uses in an entire year."[3] It's there for the taking and we'll never run out.

Solar power is the definition of a no-brainer. People are already saving money; many sell excess electricity from their rooftops back to their local utilities. But once again, entrenched monopolies are pushing back against the unknown, trying to protect market share. Some utilities have even proposed to slap fees on solar power.

Decentralization, self-reliance, competition, technological innovation, and a free market are all consistent with conservatism and a vision of true energy freedom. "Solar power is philosophically consistent with the Republican Party," said Jason Rose, a Republican public relations consultant behind the Tea Party initiative in Arizona. "If you're going to be for healthcare choice and school choice, how can you not be for energy choice? Conservatives, overwhelmingly, get that. If the Republican Party stops standing for the empowerment of the individual, what does it stand for?"[4]

Blowing relentlessly and consistently across America is wind, another source of free, clean, sustainable energy. The United States generates more wind energy than any other country except China, and wind has accounted for more than a third of all newly installed U.S. electricity generation capacity since 2007, according to the U.S. Department of Energy.[5] Today, wind powers about 5 percent of this nation's total electrical demand—more than 17 million U.S. homes annually, a twenty-five-fold increase since 2000.[6] Engineers estimate the wind blowing above U.S. coastal waters is enough to provide more than 4,000 gigawatts of electricity. That's *four* times the generating capacity of our current electric power system. During the first half of 2015, clean, renewable energy sources accounted for 70 percent of all new electrical power. The potential is enormous. We're just scratching the surface of what is possible—and inevitable.

What happens on days the wind doesn't blow or the sun doesn't shine? That's where *energy storage* comes in. New generations of powerful batteries will store electrical charge for when it's needed and provide a technological bridge to even out fluctuations in renewable energy, ensuring stable, reliable power even when the sun doesn't shine or the wind doesn't blow. Tesla's Gigafactory (highlighted in chapter 6) is set to mass produce lithium-ion batteries—the same ones in your computer, only supersized—to bring down costs so more Americans can benefit. Today, for a few thousand dollars, you can buy a Tesla Powerwall for your garage that will power your home the next time a wild storm turns out the lights—or store all the (free) energy created by the solar panels on your roof. Tesla's founder, Elon Musk, is opening up his company's patents to all competitors to accelerate clean forms of battery storage for the rest of the world.[7]

\America should take another look at nuclear energy—perhaps the only carbon-free option that can scale rapidly in the short term as we bridge the gap between dirty fossil fuels and clean, renewable sources of energy. My family lives twenty-five miles downwind of Three Mile Island, the nuclear plant near Harrisburg, Pennsylvania, that nearly melted down in 1979. Our bags were packed; we were ready to evacuate. The event was traumatizing. But my opinion of nuclear has evolved.

Mitch and I are encouraged by what we see today. Smaller, safer, more efficient forms of nuclear energy have emerged.[8] A new generation of molten salt reactors are gaining traction in the marketplace, especially in China.[9] New variations of fast neutron reactors (FNRs) are net consumers of fissile material, including plutonium. FNRs can also burn long-lived actinides, which are recovered from used fuel out of ordinary reactors.[10] Although prices are not yet cost-competitive, these new reactors can be powered by existing fuel rods sitting in storage pools around the U.S., reducing the risk of radioactive leaks and dangerous plutonium waste falling into the wrong hands. "Could all the stored nuclear waste be reused in the reactor so that there was no nuclear waste? Could the idea of a nuclear meltdown be relegated memory? Yes. There are plants operating in places around the world employing these new techniques, safely," says Twin Cities journalist and energy expert Don Shelby.[11] Nuclear power isn't perfect, but nuclear power doesn't emit greenhouse gases—and it may help to get us where we need to go, faster and at scale.

We're only scratching the surface of what's possible. Tidal energy, geothermal, biomass, biogas, and hydropower are all viable. And new innovations we can't even dream of will power the America of tomorrow. "Even without a price on carbon, technologies like electric vehicles, batteries, LED lighting, wind power, and solar power have skyrocketed in deployment and then prices drastically fall, a virtuous feedback loop," observes Michael Noble, executive director of Fresh Energy.[12] This isn't Pollyanna, pie-in-the-sky. It's the arc of technology—and American ingenuity solving a problem: We want to use more energy while paying less, *with fewer unpleasant side effects.*

Fracking opened up new reservoirs of natural gas and oil, a glut of supply depressing prices worldwide. But thanks to Moore's Law and technological advances, the price of renewables is falling even faster than the price at the gas pump.

There's a perception that dealing with climate change is a criticism of today's lifestyles, that major sacrifices will be required. The reality: We can have all the things we want and need, but do so with less stress on God's creation. You won't have to become a vegetarian, ride a bicycle to work, shave your head, or live in a yurt. This is about making smarter, cleaner, most sustainable choices as consumers.

"But dealing with climate change will kill jobs!" The reality: As we have discussed, some businesses fade as new technologies rise, creating new opportunities for reinvention, employment, and economic growth. Basing America's energy economy on dirty fuels that threaten public health in the short term, and rising seas and an accelerating cycle of weather and climate disruption for generations

to come, isn't sustainable. Base policy on what's best for our long-term economic future, not what's in the best short-term interest of habitual polluters, politicians, and the special interests that finance their political campaigns. Fixing acid rain and the ozone hole was greeted by a howl of complaints from American manufacturers, convinced at the time that tackling pollution would harm their bottom line. It never happened.

America's energy-related carbon emissions declined by 12 percent between 2005 and 2012, back to a level not seen since 1994.[13] Yes, we *can* use less dirty fuel while simultaneously growing our economy. Are we doing everything in our power to make our kids' lives safer, more secure, and more prosperous? Remaining stuck in a well-oiled carbon rut to appease entrenched monopolies ignores the lessons of history.

Addressing this challenge will fortify our coastlines and strengthen our infrastructure, making everything we do more stormproof, water-resistant, and drought-tolerant. We will develop and export the cutting-edge technologies and coping skills an anxious planet is going to need to thrive in the twenty-first century. American exceptionalism can and should apply to a cleaner, more sustainable energy future.

"The U.S. will probably not lead this parade," my father complained. "There probably has to be some natural catastrophe that clearly can be blamed on climate change. We always need something big to shock us, to wake us up. Think Pearl Harbor or 9/11."

He too was skeptical about climate change, but after spending time connecting the dots, he had his own personal *aha* moment. With climate change, everyone climbs a wall of doubt and skepticism. Some people take longer than others, but everyone is free to change their mind. There's no shame in that. Nothing less than our liberty is at stake.

This country has a long history of innovating around seemingly insurmountable obstacles. We find a creative way forward. "From the first stone tools to the invention of the electric grid, we humans have an innate drive to improve our lot through innovation. In business terms, you might consider climate change just another 'pain point' (though perhaps the mother of all 'pain points') that begs for entrepreneurs to come up with new ways of powering modern life without the pollution," said Rolf Nordstrom, president and CEO of Great Plains Institute.[14]

The symptoms of a rapidly changing climate are now showing up in the weather above our heads; visible, tangible signs that will be harder to deny as time goes on. "This isn't the climate I grew up with," says Weather Underground meteorologist Jeff Masters. "We didn't see this kind of weather in the 20th century. It's a continuation of the crazy weather we've seen over the course of the 21st century so far."[15]

The climate is changing faster than our efforts to address it. But there are concrete steps to move the needle forward. Here are a few:

1. Keep an Open Mind—and Speak Up. The changes in your yard are gradual, but weather disruption is showing up with greater regularity. Expand your horizon, keep a global perspective, monitor the changes taking place in your yard, your town, your state, and worldwide. The cancerous rise of ISIS came on suddenly, spreading far beyond Syria and Iraq. What happens "over there" can and will come back to bite us. Climate change may not be the biggest threat we face, but it will impact many other situations around the world. Food shortages, water supplies, dislocation, mass migrations, and skirmishes over remaining fossil fuel reserves will ultimately blow back on the United States, testing our military, our infrastructure, and our resolve. Global economies are intertwined and codependent. We live in our bubbles from day to day, but the symptoms of climate volatility and weather disruption don't respect international boundaries. Chances are your bubble will be popped with greater frequency and ferocity. We need to build greater resiliency into our homes, our farms, our cities, and our military.

2. Reward Efficiency. I want energy freedom—the freedom to choose the cheapest, cleanest energy alternatives available to power my home, my business, and my transportation. Fossil fuels are subsidized worldwide to the tune of $10 million every minute. That's $5.3 trillion every year. Renewable energy? A relatively paltry $120 billion every year.[16] Again, one idea is to remove— across the board—all subsidies for renewables and fossil fuels. Let the markets work. Government can set a high bar—and ensure a level playing field—but it can't pick winners. Government should be a good cop, a referee, making sure the game is played fairly. Use the marketplace to encourage innovation, technological breakthroughs, and more visionary entrepreneurs—launching the new solutions we're going to need to keep the lights on and the economy powered up, without harmful carbon pollution spiking the weather and threatening the health and welfare of your kids and their kids.

Recently, I traded in two gas-powered vehicles for an electric car with a range of two hundred miles. I charge it up in my garage every night. A small, new, energy-efficient home being planned will come with solar panels on the roof, so I can truly drive for free. That has a nice ring. *Free*. I'm not doing this because I bleed green or genuflect every time Al Gore's name is mentioned. (I don't.) I'm doing it because it's the right thing to do—and because I'll save significant money over the long-term. There's a tangible ROI. Full disclosure: I also own a RAM 1500 pickup truck, which I also love. Makes me a hypocrite, right? Perhaps. The truth: We've all benefited from fossil fuels. The day Tesla, Ford, or GM builds an electric pickup truck with a range of three hundred miles for $30,000, I'll be first in line to put down a deposit. That day is coming faster than you think.

Go out of your way to reward companies that offer energy-efficient products. It's good for the environment *and* your wallet. Consider buying energy-efficient appliances. Get an energy audit for your church, your business, and your home—you'll save energy and money over the long haul, with additional benefits. As Rolf Nordstrom says, "The clean energy transition is driven as much by consumer demand as it is the need to address climate change. In fact, we probably dwell too much on climate as a driver for energy innovation and lose sight of renewable energy's full value proposition: clean air and water, public health, jobs, stable prices, and domestic control."[17]

Why should we continue to play a subsidized game that props up countries that don't like us very much, from Saudi Arabia to Iran to Venezuela? Why is the United States the 24/7 on-call police force for the planet, ensuring the safety of supertankers and oil supply chains snaking around the world? Is there a more reliable, predictable, and responsible way to power our nation, one that doesn't see the cost of a barrel of oil collapse from $150 to $27? It's time to declare our (clean) energy independence.

3. Support a Price on Carbon Pollution. Capitalism works. It's not perfect, but it comes closest to capturing the innate spark and ambition of the human spirit. People and companies that create essential services and products should be rewarded with our business. Costs are an important part of the markets. You can't sell something profitably without knowing your total expenses. But today the true cost of carbon pollution—from health and agricultural productivity losses to property damage from super-sized floods and droughts—isn't factored into the products and services we purchase. Call me crazy, but there's nothing fair or equitable about that. It's a lopsided equation—it doesn't pass the smell test. Once there's a definable, consistent signal in the market, once we find an effective way to price carbon pollution (like we do every other form of pollution), the marketplace of ideas will react and create new-energy alternatives that emit less pollution. Government can set a high bar, but innovation and technology will create the solutions we're going to need, not some bureaucrat in Washington D.C. It's already happening, but we need to scale these inventions faster to avoid a worst-case scenario. "Climate change is the greatest wealth-generating opportunity of our lifetimes," said Sir Richard Branson, founder of Virgin Group.[18]

Disruption and reinvention is the nature of business, but entrenched monopolies will do anything to remain viable and maintain market share, delaying the inevitable. Political paralysis and orchestrated denial is slowing America's inevitable clean energy revolution, but there are creative ways to solve this vexing challenge, given courage and political will, two attributes largely lacking in politics today. We might consider a carbon fee and dividend approach, like the one proposed by Citizens' Climate Lobby:

Place a steadily rising fee on fossil fuels (coal, oil and gas).

Give all the revenue from the carbon fee back to households.

Use a border adjustment to discourage relocation.[19]

Such a plan would be *revenue neutral*. No additional money flows to the federal government; no additional layers of bureaucracy or regulatory bloat required. Return the fees to consumers or use surpluses to pay down the federal debt, an ongoing national disgrace. But let the markets work. The innovations and breakthroughs will come, and faster than we think possible. As Michael Noble, executive director at Fresh Energy, told me, "Serious and well-informed people of good will on both sides of the political divide understand that the climate challenge is more serious and more risky than we previously knew. All should agree that deploying climate solutions at scale is consistent with prosperity, equity, freedom, innovation and high standards of living. Correcting the market failure with revenue-neutral carbon pricing is consistent with free market principles."[20]

Demonize the EPA for regulating harmful pollutants? Be careful what you wish for. My family once took a vacation in China. Hoping for a leisurely bike ride through bucolic countryside, we wound up gagging on black smoke from a parade of dirty trucks. In many parts of this world you take risks when you breathe the air, drink the water, or eat the food. Other than that, things are going quite well. Is this the future we want for America? We would prefer Congress to address this issue head on through legislation, but since that hasn't happened, some appropriate level of regulation is necessary. So is finding the right *balance* of regulation—one that stimulates new economic growth while protecting the health of our kids. "Conservatives may not embrace government standards for industry, tax expenditures, and other incentives, or EPA regulations," observed Michael Noble. "These tools have been chosen by governments as proxies for the politically unachievable pricing of carbon, the only tool that would enable free markets to drive the innovation needed."[21]

We can and will figure this out.

4. Acknowledge That This Isn't a "Liberal Issue." Thermometers, ocean buoys, and satellite sensors are neither Democrat nor Republican. The data is the data. We can have a healthy respect for science while embracing our faith and protecting our earthly home. That isn't liberal spin. It's common sense. Climate science shouldn't be hijacked by political activists on the left or the right. Organizations advocating a conservative, commonsense approach to creation care and clean energy are already springing up, offering pragmatic solutions that don't grow government but rather stimulate the marketplace to invent the new tools and technologies we're going to need to adapt and thrive, no matter what a more volatile climate throws at us.

5. Elect Politicians Who Respect Science. *"I'm not a scientist"* doesn't cut it anymore. Politicians aren't economists, but they routinely vote on policies that impact the economy. Avoid the temptation to politicize science. Let's debate policy, not science. Gather data and make the best decision possible with the information at hand. That applies to scientists, and it certainly applies to the people we elect to represent our interests at a local, state, and federal level. It's in our best interest to resist the intellectual laziness of conspiracy theories and leverage the markets to invent clean alternatives, just in case the experts turn out to be right.

The tide is already turning. Consumers and companies of all sizes are investing in clean energy sources that not only clean the air, but save money, allowing them to lower costs and become more competitive. Rolf Nordstrom from Great Plains Institute adds:

> 3M is one of three large U.S. companies offering solar power as a new employee benefit, clearly seeing it as both cost-effective and a way to attract and retain talent. The chairman of M.A. Mortenson Company, the largest design-builder of wind and solar energy production in North America, said: "We can do this—we have a clear view of the clean energy system that's possible—this is no longer a science experiment or wishful thinking. And business can prosper by leading!" He would know; their solar practice has been doubling every year recently. My home state of Minnesota alone has almost as many new-energy companies as lakes.[22]

The America I know doesn't do things because they're easy. We have a reputation of engineering and innovating our way around seemingly insurmountable obstacles. The United States is uniquely positioned to address this problem and do what we do best: lead the way, exporting best practices and new technologies to the rest of the world. We are a nation of problem-solvers; we have a risk-taking mind-set and armies of entrepreneurs already focused on new, cleaner, cheaper ways to power our economy. People willing to try, tinker, fail, and get back up again and try a new route. Tenacious optimists willing to try again. Fail better.

Fail forward. There is no shame in failure. You fail until you succeed.

"Ever tried. Ever failed. No matter. Try again. Fail again. Fail better," wrote Samuel Beckett. Some of our greatest business leaders, artists, and sports stars failed repeatedly before finding success. Winston Churchill twice failed the entrance exam to military college. Henry Ford went broke five times before he succeeded. Walt Disney was fired by a newspaper editor because "he lacked imagination and had no good ideas," and then went bankrupt before building Disneyland. Michael Jordan didn't make the varsity basketball team until his junior year. What made all these people great in the end? They never gave up.

America is a land of dreamers and doers. That same roll-up-the-sleeves, get-it-done attitude will propel America into a safer, more sustainable clean-energy economy, one that employs far more people than fading fossil fuels. Even today a booming solar renaissance employs nearly three times more people than the rapidly disrupted coal industry. The impact on coal miners and their families has been devastating and heartbreaking. We share their pain. But here's a little secret: *Every* industry gets disrupted as new technologies emerge and take their place. Cars replaced the horse and buggy, telephones trumped the telegraph, and airplanes leapfrogged the railroads. It's the natural order of business. No company or individual (or politician) gets a free pass forever. The new replaces the old. Progress is painful but inevitable.

> Enlighten those who possess power and money that they may avoid the sin of indifference, that they may love the common good, advance the weak, and care for this world in which we live. The poor and the earth are crying out.[23]
>
> Pope Francis

There is cause for concern and dogged determination, but not despair. The rest of the world is looking to America for leadership.

Our elected officials take their cues from us. We worship God with our words *and our deeds*. We don't think twice about taking out insurance on our homes, our cars, and our health. Why wouldn't reasonable people take out an insurance policy on our kids and future generations? When enough people speak up, the tide will turn. The result will be true energy freedom and a sustainable economy that inspires and empowers the rest of the world.

"We'll need legions of risk-takers, big thinkers, innovators, engineers, entrepreneurs, and smart business people to create a low emissions society. We can't do it without them. And at the end of the path will be a society with a stable climate, no dependence on foreign oil, no oil spills, no coal mining accidents, and far less air and water pollution. A better world is waiting for us to create it," said Stanford University's Jonathan Koomey.[24]

The symptoms of a warming climate will become more frequent and glaring in the years to come. We're just seeing the tip of a (rapidly melting) iceberg. The trends will become harder to deny. I'm no prophet. Most days I'm a naïve optimist and puzzled spectator, connecting dots, looking for trends. But here is what I do know: We love our kids. We want to protect them. Keep them safe. Give them every opportunity to succeed. Life is tough enough. Why would we make it any harder on them? *"This is too difficult." "It's too expensive." "America can't solve this problem." "Oh, and good luck, kids! Sorry we looked the other way. Made excuses. Took the easy way out."* Is this our legacy?

"No man was ever honored for what he received. Honor has been the reward for what he gave," said Calvin Coolidge. What are we leaving our kids and all those who come next? We are here to worship our Creator and enjoy the fruits of his creation during our fleeting time on his earth. We are stewards of a very precious gift. Everything around us is on loan; we don't really *own* anything—we're just passing through, as Billy Graham preached: "My home is in heaven. I'm just traveling through this world."

WWJD. What would Jesus do? I don't pretend to know. He might nod his head and smile as he takes in the incomprehensible genius of his Father's creation. *"Did you protect my Father's home? Did you defend his children?"*

What will we tell him?

CHAPTER 8

We Can Do It—
With God's Help

May the God of hope fill you with all joy and peace as you trust in him, so that you may overflow with hope by the power of the Holy Spirit.

Romans 15:13

For eighteen years, I (Mitch) carried the Romans 15 verse on each calling card given to new folks attending worship or dropped off as neighbors were visited or hospital calls were made. This Scripture conveys my belief in who God is and the hope only Jesus provides. It's why I'm hopeful about the future. By working together with God as our guide, we can rebuild our land with unpolluted air, pure water, healthy kids, and good jobs powered by new energies. All of which can also be shared with all of God's children around the world.

Government can't do it, businesses can't go it alone, and we won't be able to do it by ourselves. But we can do it together.

I know, easier said than done. Sadly, there's too little common ground for the common good or compassion for our neighbors. Maybe we need to reread the Good Samaritan parable over and over again. Far too often, we act like the good "church" folk who walked by the injured man instead of the outcast who stopped to help.

My greatest satisfaction as a local church pastor was seeing churches come together to build God's kingdom. I use the word *church* hesitantly because the first thing a group of twelve or so pastors did several years ago in my hometown was stop using the word *church* to refer to a particular congregation or even a denomination. We agreed that there is only one Church, and we are but a part of God's work as congregations.

The inspiration for these congregations working jointly was a sermon preached by Jim Cymbala at a National Pastors Conference years ago in San Diego. With a bit of paraphrasing, Pastor Jim said, "Brooklyn Tabernacle is in the heart of the 'hood. We could do a million different ministries, but we can't do it all. We do what God has called us to do, and *trust* in God that other congregations will accomplish the ministries set before them."

These local congregations, including evangelicals, Pentecostals, and even a couple mainlines, stopped worrying about theological differences and scriptural interpretations and put our focus on being Jesus for the world. We understood that each congregation had different gifts, but those gifts would both connect with different people and empower different ministries. Together we celebrated a win for God if one congregation helped someone start their relationship with Jesus while another helped the same person to grow with God. No more worries about "church hopping" or competition. If members of one congregation were needed to rebuild a home, we encouraged and empowered each other's ministries. One of the most powerful witnesses happened on a Christmas Eve, as each congregation united to share the same message topic, "Jesus Beyond the Box," in their own voice. The theme was simple: Jesus came to go beyond the institutional religion of the day and offer a living, relevant faith.

We need to not only get out of the box but go beyond it. It is my hope that the church will be the leader, bringing people together to care for creation, defend our kids, and rekindle our can-do spirit. It's happened before and it can happen again. We must accept the reality of our changing climate and simply work together. We need to mobilize a national effort to offer new hope and new opportunities, a common purpose to make our lives and our nation stronger.

Fortunately, we have a model created in York County, Pennsylvania, as an example. As the realization of World War II hit America in February 1942, a group of York business and community leaders gathered and drafted the York Plan.[1] The fifteen-point plan called for shared expertise; sought cooperation (not competitiveness) and joint resources; and campaigned for health, housing, and fair wages for all. The York Plan, adapted quickly for national use, provided the blueprint for our society coming together to find solutions, work in harmony, remain competitive, and value employees. We need to rekindle at least the concept of the York Plan to defend our kids and their future. Our suggestion might never gain the structure of the York Plan, but it involves all of us. It starts with us as individuals, moves to our local communities, and ends with national policies that can move our nation in the right direction.

Us and Our Families

It does start with us, and nowhere is that more important than to us conservatives! I remember one of my early presentations on climate change. I discussed several actions, and after sharing, one gentleman said, "You're the first person who ever said I could make a difference as an individual." Another man said, "We do have a biblical responsibility as stewards, and I am going to change my farming practice to reduce my fertilizer use and my carbon footprint."

Not all of us have three thousand acres like a farmer, but each of us can reduce our carbon footprint while saving money. Additional conservation ideas and information can be found at creationcare .org and pauldouglasweather.com, but I want to share a few specific points here.

Don't rush out and buy a new hybrid or an electric car if your current car still works well. But when you do need to purchase another vehicle, choose the most energy-efficient vehicle for your family. If you have three kids and two pets, you may need a mini-van. Go with what works and saves energy. Electric cars are quickly becoming the next generation, and perhaps hydrogen fuel cells are another future possibility. While Teslas are still pricey, other all-electric or plug-in cars are quickly becoming cost competitive. A side note: Teslas are the most American-made automobile, and they're fun to drive! A pastor friend invited me to drive his Model S a few months ago. As we left the congregation's facility, he tossed me the keys and said, "You drive." We then proceeded to a freeway on-ramp, where I was told to "punch it." Let's just say I was more than surprised when the acceleration almost tossed me into the backseat.

Right now energy efficiency remains the most effective way to be good stewards in both money and carbon. The smart thing is not to trash refrigerators or air-conditioners in good working order (but if they're more than ten years old it's probably worth it). When purchasing the next generation, buy the highest Energy Star appliance possible. A personal experience: We replaced our older, inefficient gas furnace two years ago, and while it was more expensive to replace it with an ultra-high-efficiency unit, the payback is already almost complete. Another good energy-efficient idea is to check your insulation and repair leaks around windows and doors, etc. A few dollars spent can return immediate savings.

Installing your own solar, geothermal, or other cleaner energies can help defend our children and save money too. As discussed previously, renewable energy prices continue to fall, and many homeowners can take advantage of clean energy and lower prices, with the added benefit of having the freedom to choose their electricity. Of course, some utilities continue to fight this opportunity and preserve their monopolist business model. This is unfortunate and troubling. Every American should have the freedom and independence to choose electric suppliers. It's simply unpatriotic to do otherwise.

Renewables are not just for the affluent. Even lower-income folks can take advantage of various opportunities. In Pennsylvania, Texas, New England, and a handful of other states, individuals can choose their electric supplier. Pennsylvania has PA Switch, an online way to select different sources and suppliers of electricity. Currently, I purchase 100 percent wind-produced electricity at roughly the price of coal-generated power. And if one factors the hidden costs of coal buried in our kids' brains and lungs, it's an invaluable economic advantage for all of us.

Businesses are also leading the way in lowering the cost of solar. One shining example is PosiGen, located in Louisiana and now spreading to New York, Connecticut, and Florida. This firm has thousands of solar installations and provides a combination of leased or purchased solar systems.

Leasing or owning your own solar panels is just one way. A growing and significant new market of renewables is known as community-based solar (CBS). Only 22 to 27 percent of U.S. homes are suitable for solar.[2] The percentage is limited by the number of those who rent or lease, not because of sunlight availability. In reality, approximately 50 percent of American buildings are suitable for solar, but CBS offers an additional opportunity to take advantage and control of your energy.

Community-based solar, using economies of scale (the bigger the system, the lower per-unit cost), can operate in a number of ways.

Apartment or industrial complexes could operate their own systems. A housing development, town, or neighborhood may do the same. Even congregations or businesses might install larger systems than required for their needs and sell the excess to neighbors.

This mini-grid basis for supplying surrounding homes affords cost saving here and in the developing world. In Guatemala, for example, grid-supplied electricity already costs 18 to 20 cents per kilowatt, and solar power can provide much less expensive electricity at a guaranteed price for twenty years. Photovoltaic panels don't degrade over time and the majority of manufacturers guarantee their output over twenty years, thus ensuring a constant price. As most of us know from our bills, utility-driven electricity has not remained constant for the last twenty years. But today is a new day. The electricity market is rapidly changing worldwide, and we can enjoy the change or remain the same.

One limiting factor to CBS is current laws and regulations. Florida, for instance, has a law on its books that prevents anyone or any business to sell electricity other than regulated utilities. Consumer advocates have for years attempted to have the Florida Legislature amend the statute, without success. However, there is a current movement to place an energy freedom initiative on the Florida ballot and allow Floridians to make the choice.

The choice exists for all us. Each of us can take responsibility for our energy use, our energy efficiency, and other more subtle acts of stewardship. No one can tell another person how to live or what car to drive, or even how to live in fellowship with both God and neighbor. However, the saying "What would Jesus do?" comes to mind.

I grew up and live out my faith in the Wesleyan tradition. John Wesley understood grace to work in each of us in three ways. First, in classic Wesley language, is "prevenient grace." It's Jesus going before us in every aspect of life and making us aware of our mistakes, our faults, and our broken relationships. And in the moment we understand ourselves as not perfect, as not living in the image of God for which we were created, and if we ask for reconciliation with God and ultimately each other, we are forgiven. In the moment of forgiveness, grace acts to justify us (align us with God) or restore us to the right relationship, but our journey doesn't end with forgiveness. Each of us is called to follow Jesus, to act more like him, and in fact be Jesus or at least the image of God for the world. We are not left alone in our walk. Jesus guides us each step of the way and is with us in what Wesley would call "sanctifying grace." While theological disputes continue on whether our "holiness" happens immediately, over time, or not at all, there is common agreement that discipleship means growing more like Christ. It's also true that alternate views within the church discuss whether or not grace is resistible. Calvin and, before him, Eusebius (an early church father), described the three offices of Jesus as Prophet, Priest, and King. The prophet who calls us to account; the priest, who through sacrifice provides forgiveness; and the king, who has established his kingdom and calls his followers to join in.

The point is, no matter what your theology, we have a choice and a decision to make. More than a matter of dollars and cents, caring for God's creation is a biblical imperative — it's about living rightly with God and each other. So the question each of us must answer for ourselves is, "What is Jesus calling us to do in caring for our kids, their future, and what Pope Francis calls our 'common home'?"

Our Local Congregations and Community

Just as energy efficiency is the smartest idea for our homes, so it is with our congregations and their buildings. Around six years ago, I helped facilitate a study by the National Renewable Energy Laboratory (NREL) to analyze energy efficiency possibilities in houses of worship. The results of the study were turned into the

Energy Star Action Workbook for Congregations. The workbook, downloadable from energystar.gov, provides a good starting point for congregations wishing to save money and be good stewards.

The study found that almost all congregations can save about 5 percent of their energy use by performing simple tasks like weather stripping, caulking, and increased insulation. Greater savings can be accomplished with changing lights, zone controls, or equipment replacement. What's important is the starting point. Whether you begin with a free resource like the Energy Star workbook or hire an energy auditor, you can save energy, lower operating costs, and become better caretakers.

Some of the results can be dramatic. Prestonwood Baptist Church in Plano, Texas, saved approximately 33 percent on their energy bill. The headquarters of the Christian Reformed Church in Grand Rapids, Michigan, saved over $544,000 in recouped energy costs in the first three years and is now encouraging all their congregations to conduct energy efficiency studies. Both facilities bear the Energy Star label, and other worship facilities across the nation are following their leadership.

For the church, energy efficiency is not just about saving money or even creation care. Modeling energy efficiency educates members and their local communities on the possibilities, and it also allows the saved energy resources to be directed into new ministries. Many churches struggle for finances; what could be a better way to model discipleship than saving scarce resources and turning them into other opportunities?

"Lighting Up the World in the Name of the Light of the World" is the name EEN's initiative by which congregations pass on part of their energy savings funds to mission organizations like New Vision Renewal Energy.[3] New Vision supplies solar lights to orphanages and others in the majority world, teaches congregations how to build and install their own renewable energy, and works to retrain workers in the midst of Appalachia.

Even large Christian relief and development agencies are becoming aware of renewable energy. After decades of limited engagement, development organizations are beginning to support and encourage energy development. The first venture for many was the introduction of healthier cookstoves of various designs. Solar or high-efficiency stoves continue to reduce both loss of life from indoor air pollution and prevent forest depletion. Although some have questioned the benefit of clean cookstoves, these programs have started a movement for clean energy.

Many still live in a paradigm of central electric generation stations and massive transmission networks. Both were and still are cost prohibitive for the majority world, and therefore unrealistic. Until recently. Renewable energy changes everything. That said, we don't support unsustainable programs. We strongly believe in the old axiom, "Teaching people how to fish is better than providing the fish." Clean energy needs to be an investment, not a handout. Our recommendation: Use energy savings to fund investment in loan programs that can continually support market or cooperative clean energy programs around the world.

On a smaller scale, there are many ministries related to creation care that help mitigate climate change, increase awareness, build community, and help others closer to our homes. The Joseph Pledge (presented below), community gardens, and even making your own laundry detergent all reinforce the biblical imperative to care for creation, reduce carbon pollution, and build community.

The Joseph Pledge

The Joseph Pledge is based on the Genesis patriarch Joseph, who prepared Egypt for disasters. The pledge calls on each local evangelical community to take creation care seriously and prepare for local disasters and the ever-increasing threats from extreme weather.

We encourage congregations to sign the pledge that follows and take action within their community.

Public health professionals warn that extreme weather causes increased risks. Heart attacks, heat casualties, and respiratory illness, caused by heat waves or massive snowstorms, are exacerbated. Be proactive and have a plan to rescue those in need. Know members of your congregations as well as others in need and where they live. Have a volunteer team ready to rescue or to call emergency responders as needed to transport them to heating or cooling centers. Congregations can prepare their buildings as shelters or work together with other churches to ensure adequate emergency facilities with sound structure, supplies, energy, and staff.

Here's just one story: After preaching at a local church on climate change and our biblical response, a good-sized man in a wheelchair approached me and shared how he almost died in his second-floor apartment. Existing on disability and with a number of health problems, the gentleman had limited income and no air conditioning. During a heat wave where daytime temperatures exceeded ninety degrees for over a week, the man became dehydrated, lost consciousness, and fell from his wheelchair. He laid there for over twenty-four hours until a concerned neighbor forced her way into his apartment and called 9-1-1, saving his life with only minutes to spare.

The elderly, people with disabilities, and those with lower incomes are already more adversely impacted by disasters and severe weather. We only need to remember Superstorm Sandy or Hurricane Katrina as recent examples.

Disasters have occurred since the beginning of recorded time: famine, floods, extreme weather, economic recessions, pandemics, and other natural and man-made crises. While disasters cause tragic suffering and loss of life, they also draw us into deeper dependence on God as we seek to protect our families and care for our neighbors.

The Bible teaches us two things about dealing with crises. The first is to prepare for unexpected times ahead, having a plan of action to address both spiritual and physical needs. The second is to use our resources to help our neighbor, the poor, widows, the unborn, orphans, and the vulnerable.

Churches and Christians should be leading the way in our communities when a crisis does occur, working alongside our neighbors and our government leaders. Joseph was not part of a church or religious community. He was part of the Egyptian government. God had placed him there. You never know who God may have placed in your local government to help your church get prepared and offer solutions when there is a need.

The Joseph Pledge

With God's help, we commit to preparing our congregation for extreme weather events so that we can protect our families and serve our community when disaster strikes, by doing the following:

1. Affirming creation care as a matter of life, and accepting our biblical responsibility as a steward of all that God has entrusted to me/us

2. Preparing our church building(s) for extreme weather and cooperating with other local congregations to offer shelter for the most vulnerable among us

3. Establishing a congregational task force, if needed, to develop and implement plans and procedures to be followed when a natural disaster occurs

4. Encouraging our members to maintain a supply of emergency food, water, and medical supplies

5. Identifying, locating, and planning relocation transport for our most at-risk neighbors

6. Coordinating efforts with local governments, emergency responders, and disaster relief services, and establishing a clear communications plan

7. Training a team of volunteers to assist with spiritual and emotional stress during extreme weather events

8. Implementing a regularly scheduled training session for the congregation for extreme weather

9. Maintaining energy-efficient church buildings and operations, using the *Energy Star Action Workbook for Congregations* or other appropriate resources

10. Encouraging our members to advocate for public policies that preserve and renew God's creation, defend our children now, and provide hope for the future[4]

Creation care shouldn't be all doom and gloom. Yes, there's plenty of gloom, but as evangelical Christians, we are called to live our lives in the hope provided as a direct result of Jesus' resurrection—trusting and anticipating that the ultimate fulfillment of God's kingdom is the ultimate reality for life on earth.

My friend Tim Olson leads an outstanding ministry in Sioux Falls, South Dakota, called Ground Works-Midwest that lives into hope.[5] Tim and his team specialize in community teaching gardens for elementary schools, churches, and other nonprofits. They demonstrate urban farming to children who have never seen lettuce grow or known where a carrot comes from. Their work provides healthy food that's locally sourced, providing new possibilities in healthy living and caring for God's creation. (The more local food we produce or purchase reduces carbon pollution associated with transportation.)

Ground Works is one of many organizations and local churches either operating community gardens as a fresh food source for low-income families or providing low-cost land for community members to have their own gardens. Another great example is Harrisonburg Mennonite Church in Harrisonburg, Virginia. They have hosted a community garden for years. Every spring they rent out small plots for a nominal fee, including water. It's amazing to visit their garden on a summer evening. You can see wonderful and unique vegetables from all over the world as new immigrants grow some of their favorite plants in this amazing garden. In addition to the community garden, the congregation has a beautiful prayer walk that traverses their property. Designed by Dr. Anne Nielsen, a retired biology professor, the prayer journey has wonderful stops for prayer and reflections—all of which is surrounded by beautiful and very intentional indigenous plants. They also have one of the most active creation care teams and are a model to us all.

Another food stewardship issue is food waste. According to the United Department of Agriculture, one in seven households is "food insecure" (they don't have enough to eat) and almost 15 percent of U.S. homes lack regular access to diets that support an active healthy lifestyle. At the same time, we are tossing 34.5 million tons of food waste into landfills or other disposal means. The food thrown into landfills decomposes into methane that is a greenhouse gas 86 times more potent than carbon dioxide in the first twenty years. In simple terms, if we could eliminate the food waste going into landfills, it would be like taking 25 percent of all cars off American roads.

We recommend a few simple ministries to address both feeding those who are hungry and reducing methane pollution. First, whether for a church meal or at home, prepare only the needed amount. Donate any leftovers to a local shelter or other accepting organization. A small group can also arrange with local restaurants to "pick-up" leftovers and deliver to those in need. Finally, for remaining non-meat leftovers, organize a composting location around the church. The compost makes great soil for a community garden or for the church community at large.

Another simple and practical creation care activity that builds community is making laundry detergent. The "recipe" I got from my millennial-age daughter is easy, inexpensive, healthy—and it works. You can find several different formulas online or on the EEN website, and it only requires a home or church kitchen, a group of volunteers, and a few dollars to make a month's worth of detergent.

Energy efficiency, extreme weather preparedness, and safe, non-toxic cleaning products are just a few of the thousands of ways we can work together to make a difference. By themselves, however, they won't be enough. Some of the greatest problems are systemic to our way of life and have been ingrained in our social norms, our markets, and even our government. So our work and ministry won't be complete unless we push and support policy actions at the local, state, and federal levels.

Conservatives, including Paul and I, recognize that government isn't the answer for everything. We as individuals must act and take responsibility for our actions. However, sometimes we forget that our government is *us*. Our Constitution begins with the line "We the People." Our government reflects who we are collectively as a complete nation. A democratically elected representative government certainly isn't perfect, but our American system has endured for almost 250 years, and hopefully, if we the people live out our faith, represent our values, and act to hold our government (us) accountable in Christ's love, it will last another 250 years or whenever Christ returns.

The Evangelical Environmental Network ministry includes sharing our biblical understanding of creation care with our federal government in Washington and with many state governments as well. It's an important ministry, validated by both the Lausanne Movement (founded by Billy Graham and John Stott) and the National Association of Evangelicals. Our team represents 2.5 million (and growing) pro-life Christians from around our nation, who have taken action to support policies to defend our children and steward God's creation.

Unfortunately, many people have an us-versus-government attitude. Without doubt, our government includes folks who understand God as we do. It also includes those who profess Christianity with different beliefs from ours, some with different faiths, and others with no faith at all. In other words, those in government look like the folks in the grocery store. They look like our communities and are as diverse as our towns. They are just like us, because they are us. They are God's children, created in his image, whether or not they acknowledge it. And the most important witness we and the church can accomplish is representing Jesus and his love. Even with my mistakes and foibles, my most important gift is being a unique person, saved by grace and called to ministry in Christ's service. The Scripture that most reflects my calling to ordained ministry comes from Hebrews:

> Every high priest is selected from among the people and is appointed to represent the people in matters related to God, to offer gifts and sacrifices for sins. He is able to deal gently with those who are ignorant and are going astray, since he himself is subject to weakness. This is why he has to offer sacrifices for his own sins, as well as for the sins of the people. And no one takes this honor on himself, but he receives it when called by God, just as Aaron was.
>
> Hebrews 5:1–4

A long time ago I learned to be gentle on the sins of others because of my own sins, and my sons have a wonderful way to remind me. "Remember, Dad, you're a pastor, not a saint" has become part of me. The cue, paraphrased from the 2002 film version of *The Count of Monte Cristo*, helps me recall that none of us are perfect. It's not that sin is irrelevant, but not one of us has a right to the "holier than thou" attitude. In so many cases in public policy and discourse, however, we seem to have forgotten our need for grace. In an earlier chapter, I mentioned the meeting between President Obama and Pope Francis. If we are going to move forward as a nation, many of us will need a fresh infusion of grace, mercy, and love. It's not that we must give up on who we are or reject our theology or our core values, but we must use God's grace and love to empower us to move forward and overcome climate change *using* our values and validating the beliefs of others.

Public Policy

Our government can't do it, businesses can't go it alone, and we won't be able to do it by ourselves. But we can do it together. It's time to bring all the pieces together and trust God that everyone will do their part, including government. Before actually sharing the recommended policy actions, I want to relay a few separate but related events.

Once, during a United States Senate Environment and Public Works Committee hearing on mercury pollution, Senator Lamar Alexander (R-TN) stated words to the effect that the government needed to set the limits and allow the industry to figure out the way to meet the standards. Senator Alexander, who I regard as one of our great statesmen, was saying government (us) needed to set levels that ensure our rights as addressed by our early patriots, who wrote:

> We hold these truths to be self-evident, that all men are created equal, that they are endowed by their Creator with certain unalienable Rights, that among these are Life, Liberty and the pursuit of Happiness. — That to secure these rights, Governments are instituted among Men, deriving their just powers from the consent of the governed. . . .
>
> The Declaration of Independence, 1776

We all have rights, but actions that tread on the rights of others stand against who we are as evangelicals and Americans. No industry or individual has the right to interfere with basic God-given rights, and polluting our kids with toxins and emitting gases that change our climate to the detriment of all interfere with our unalienable rights. Our government's responsibility embedded in the Declaration of Independence and our Constitution preserve our "rights" to breathe, have healthy brains, and pursue our dreams without a warming earth that steals our security and our ability to prosper.

It's our government's role to set the rules to empower all of us to live by the standards called for in the Bible.

> He has shown you, O mortal, what is good.
>   And what does the Lord require of you?
> To act justly and to love mercy
>   and to walk humbly with your God.
>   Micah 6:8

Businesses desire the same level playing field, notwithstanding their public rhetoric. Recently, I helped facilitate a discussion between EPA officials and the natural gas industry on upcoming methane leak standards. Despite the rhetoric often spoken by industry groups, not one firm in the room objected to the proposed rule. The gas industries' desire is to be provided with a performance regulation and be given the freedom to utilize their technology, as only they have the knowledge to do, to effectively meet those criteria. Their comments make sense and closely align with Senator Alexander's statements.

The industry quietly supports the standard, and it makes everyone play by the same rules. Imagine a football game where the two teams and the referees have different expectations. It would be chaos. It would be wonderful if everyone agreed to play "nice," but sin sooner or later distorts fairness.

In the natural gas industry, research states that approximately 80 percent of the natural gas leaks result from 30 percent of the facilities.[6] That suggests that many producers already see the value in minimizing leaks and production losses. Escaping natural gas can't make a profit, but it can be extremely toxic and of immeasurable harm to our children's health.

It also indicates that lower-cost operators without proper care or without sound capitalization operate on the margins. While being sympathetic to the small businessperson, the current threats to children's health demand proper accountability. Supporting this new standard creates, in effect, a police force to ensure our kids' health.

Good policy acts like law enforcement and protects our "rights" to life, liberty, and the pursuit of happiness while poor policy hinders those same rights. Throughout this book, we have explained that fossil fuels have had the benefit of the greatest "corporate welfare" of all time. Beginning in 1916, the petroleum industry has been provided tax breaks, subsidies, and other benefits that certainly are not market based and don't reflect conservative values. Just as important and discussed at length previously, the true costs of fossil fuels have been borne by our children's health instead of the market.

Basic economic principle states that if something costs more, it's used less. In the case of fossil fuels, the costs are hidden and we have no way to judge value and therefore no way to choose alternatives. Hidden costs protect one market and hinder new market development, further shifting reality. Correcting market failure to ensure our basic rights is both conservative and just.

We have spent considerable effort previously in calling for an end to subsidies; now we will share two possibilities to address hidden costs. The first is what's commonly called *command and control* or even more simply, *regulation*. The second is a pollution fee.

The Environmental Protection Agency has recently finalized standards for both new and existing coal-fired power plants. Using the authority of the Clean Air Act renewed under President George H. W. Bush, the Clean Power Plan, as it's called, sets limits for carbon pollution and requires each state to develop a State Implementation Plan (SIP) for reducing pollution (from electricity generation) that works best for each state. The Evangelical Environmental Network has strongly supported this effort. We generated over 230,000 comments in support of the Clean Power Plan from pro-life Christians and organized a letter of support to President Obama with over 130 evangelical leaders' signatures. Part of the letter reads:

> As evangelical leaders from across the country we write to commend you for your leadership on climate change. We see overcoming the climate challenge as one of the great moral opportunities of our time, a chance to fulfill the Great Commandments to love God, our neighbors, and ourselves. It is God's love that calls all of us to take on this challenge. That is why we write to offer our support and encouragement for your efforts to overcome the climate challenge.
>
> Your leadership is laid out in your Climate Action Plan, which, when fully implemented, will (1) position America to lead the world in the coming clean energy revolution, (2) create good jobs here in America, (3) reduce pollution that fouls our air and makes our water impure, (4) protect the health of our children and the unborn, and (5) build resiliency to the consequences of climate change both here and in vulnerable poor nations.
>
> Like you, we would much prefer that Congress act to reduce carbon pollution through a market-based approach, such as a revenue-neutral carbon tax swap that cuts other taxes. Until they do, we are grateful that you have stepped up to fill this leadership vacuum, because time is of the essence.
>
> A key part of your climate effort is the Environmental Protection Agency's (EPA's) Clean Power Plan (CPP), which for the first time requires electric utilities to reduce carbon pollution from existing power plants. The CPP is an essential step, the most important one we will have made to date in overcoming climate change. More than anything it shows our nation's resolve, that our journey has now begun in earnest

and there's no turning back. This by itself will spur innovation and investment in the marketplace. We are glad to add our voices to the nearly 230,000 pro-life Christians who have contacted the EPA in support of the CPP.[7]

The Clean Power Plan isn't perfect, but it's a step in the right direction. Still, it only addresses carbon pollution in one industry and requires other industries to be addressed in separate regulations. It's inefficient and potentially more costly than market-based approaches, but it's the only option, with Congress failing to act. Action is required before it's too late. As the letter states, we would rather have Congress act, and that's where the market correction factor possibility exists.

The regulation alternative that's supported by many conservative economists, business leaders, and even oil companies is a carbon pollution fee or carbon tax. It's highly efficient and market driven, but it has one major problem: the word *tax*. When most

The Conservative Case for a Carbon Tax

Costly and economically inefficient command-and-control greenhouse gas regulations are firmly entrenched in law, and there is no plausible scenario in which they can be removed by conservative political force. Even were that not the case, the risks imposed by climate change are real, and a policy of ignoring those risks and hoping for the best is inconsistent with risk-management practices conservatives embrace in other, non-climate contexts. Conservatives should embrace a carbon tax (a much less costly means of reducing greenhouse gas emissions) in return for elimination of EPA regulatory authority over greenhouse gas emissions, abolition of green energy subsidies and regulatory mandates, and offsetting tax cuts to provide for revenue neutrality.[8]

Jerry Taylor, president of the Niskanen Center

Conservatives don't support tax increases that are veiled as "cap and trade" schemes for pollution permits. But offer us a tax swap, and we could become the . . . best allies on climate change.[9]

Bob Inglis, former U.S. Representative, and Arthur Laffer, conservative economist

conservatives hear that word, there's a visceral reaction. Not many like the thought of government taking more money from our pockets. Helping people to understand that it's different from a traditional "tax" will be difficult, but it's the right thing to do. Carbon pollution fees or taxes as offered by most economists are not designed to go into the Treasury's coffers but rather be a neutral revenue stream. While called a fee or tax, it's really an adjustment to the hidden costs we've been paying all along. It's not a perfect analogy, but a "loss leader," otherwise known as a bait-and-switch, is when a product is advertised at below cost to entice people into a store in order for them to purchase more or another item. In a real sense, fossil fuels have been loss leaders for over a century, and it's time to pay up. The biggest difference in the analogy is that instead of the seller being held accountable for any losses, the consumer has paid the loss in external costs while the seller has made the profits.

There are slightly different pollution-fee variations floating in the media, offered by think tanks, and even one current piece of legislation. The most effective way of levying a carbon tax is by charging as far "upstream" as possible. For coal, that's at the mine. For oil or natural gas, it's either at the well, collection point, or refinery; if the fuel is imported, tax it at the port. Most experts suggest a starting point of $16 per ton of carbon, which translates into approximately 16 cents per gallon of gasoline and increasing approximately 5 percent per year. The fee would also be assessed as a border correction (tariff) on products produced outside the

There are plenty of solutions that will appeal to conservatives and make good sense. A deregulated electricity sector that allowed consumers everywhere to pick their own power companies and generate their own power seems like a winning issue. So does a redirection of corporate-welfare subsidies into true basic energy research on potential breakthroughs.[10]

Eli Lehrer, president of R Street Institute

United States and not already assessed as a carbon correction factor in order to protect jobs and industry.

Most conservative leaders discussing and supporting a carbon fee acknowledge they must be revenue neutral. In simple terms, that means the fee must offset other taxes, be rebated to consumers, or some combination of both. What appears to be the popular choice with economists is using the funds to reduce our corporate tax rate and the balance returned to consumers on a scale similar to current income tax. In other words, those in lower income brackets would receive close to a 100 percent rebate, while higher income brackets would see proportional reduced returns. If you wish to learn more on carbon taxes as a conservative opportunity, please read "The Conservative Case for a Carbon Tax"[11] by Jerry Taylor from the respected Niskanen Center. (An excerpt from that report is in the sidebar story a few pages back.) Another worthy read is "How to Tax Carbon: Conservatives Can Fight Climate Change Without Growing Government" by Andrew Moylan in the October 2, 2013 issue of *The American Conservative*.[12]

There is no doubt that our current fuel policy is unfair and unjust. It's quite honestly a travesty of both fiscal conservatism and evangelical values. We simply can't continue to subsidize fossil fuels with the health and life of our children. It's simply not caring for life. We have a choice. Is it right to save a few dollars at the gas pump or on our electric bill to poison our kids? I don't believe so, especially when investing in clean energy will save lives, offer better opportunities, and in the end build a better economy for the same children we are currently denying abundant life. It's time to be fair and invest in a kingdom-of-God future that values opportunities for all God's children and supports a fair economic system.

Investing in our nation and its future provides the best prospect for going forward. All of us must make the effort; it's a faithful call to action. But just transforming the mistakes of the past won't get us where we need to go. Overcoming climate change requires new thinking and going beyond the box, just like God did when he came to earth at Christmas.

In his incarnation, Jesus invested in humanity. He modeled the right way for living; he sought new paradigms in relationships, and in his death and resurrection initiated something completely new: the kingdom of God. Jesus provided a new vision for his disciples to grasp, and he went before them to show them the new way.

Bill Gates is known as the richest man in the world. In a 2014 interview, he talked about attending a Catholic church with his wife.

> The mystery and the beauty of the world is overwhelmingly amazing, and there's no scientific explanation of how it came about. To say that it was generated by random numbers, that does seem, you know, sort of an uncharitable view. I think it makes sense to believe in God, but exactly what decision in your life you make differently because of it, I don't know.[13]

I like to believe God is working in Mr. Gates, not only because of his philanthropy, but for his inspired vision for the future. Mr. Gates has called for a massive increase in U.S. government research for clean energy—three times the current rate of funding.[14, 15]

Government shouldn't be in the occupation of picking energy business winners or losers. But investing in basic research is for the common good. These investments have paid big dividends, from

> The United States has a historically unmatched record—as the American Energy Innovation Council's recent case studies show—of successful energy RD&D. America's national laboratories, which have no peer in the world, have birthed hundreds of technologies that today dominate the global energy market. U.S. RD&D investments have created the world's best natural gas turbines, the most sophisticated oil-drilling equipment, the world's most efficient solar cells, advanced glass and lighting, and much more. The costs of this RD&D are tiny compared with the benefits. But today's investments are simply too small: they will not offer an expanded range of economic, security, and environmental options in the future.
>
> American Energy Innovation Council

space programs to the Internet. No one company could do it—but we can do it together. The possibilities are endless, from nanotechnologies remaking home appliances or complete automobiles manufactured entirely by 3-D printers. Investment in ourselves will change how the world uses energy, rekindle our economy, defeat climate change, and improve the lives of our children. We can rekindle the American spirit without costing us a dime by merely redirecting just a few of those hundred-year-old fossil fuel subsidies.

The investment accelerates solving climate change, thereby reducing risks to our nation, our kids, and the poor around the world. This investment can and probably will provide the energy supply needed for development all around the world and the ability to preserve our common home for the next generation. The possibilities are endless, but we must be willing to follow our risen Lord.

Our Vision

We see cleaner skies and purer water, healthy children free to enjoy the beauty of God's creation, their bodies not hindered by pollution, their brains not diminished by toxins. We see an economy that is the envy of the world, producing the technologies that help us achieve life, liberty, and happiness. We see technologies that lead to a cleaner environment and plentiful, affordable energy to power our homes, vehicles, and businesses. We envision technologies that provide us free time for family and loved ones so that we can rebuild community life and be creative with the gifts God has given each of us, technology that creates clean energy that empowers sustainable economic progress and lifts billions out of poverty and into prosperity.

Leaders of our past—Lincoln, Teddy Roosevelt, Edison, Martin Luther King Jr., Steve Jobs—dared to think big and achieved great things that make our lives better today. Let's be inspired by their example and not make the mistake of thinking small, caving to fear, and returning to our "Egypt." As God's children, we are no longer slaves to fear, climate change, or dirty energy. Let's truly care for creation.

It's a matter of life.

Acknowledgments

From Mitch Hescox

Many of the thoughts, ideas, and concepts in this manuscript originated from within the best ministry team ever. Without the efforts of the Evangelical Environmental Network's staff, especially Jim Ball and Alexei Laushkin, my portion's content would be shallow indeed. Any faults, failures, or missteps remain my responsibility, but their wisdom, knowledge, and friendship have been an inspiration to my life and ministry with EEN. Additional special thanks goes to my first editor and older son, Aaron, who took my rambling efforts and turned them into a solid manuscript. Thank you to Dawn Frederick, Red Sofa Literary, and Jeff Braun, Bethany House Publishers, for taking chance on us, and to the mastermind of this project Paul Douglas, my partner.

From Paul Douglas

Life (and publishing) is like the weather. You never know exactly how it's going to turn out. I didn't set out to write a book about a conservative approach to tackling climate change. Things just fell into place; the culmination of twenty years of tracking increasingly strange and troubling weather patterns on my maps.

First and foremost, a big thank you to my friend, colleague, and coauthor, Reverend Mitch Hescox. We met in Washington, D.C. several years ago, and I was immediately struck by his faith, commitment, and passion. Mitch and his team at EEN have been focused on the short-term impacts of fossil fuels on human health, with a growing awareness that climate change will pose an escalating risk for generations to come, especially among those with the least—the very people Jesus commanded us to love and protect. We both agree that we honor the Creator when we honor his creation. Hurricane Mitch is a force of nature, and I'm proud to call him my friend.

Conservatives are stepping up and acknowledging the obvious in increasing numbers. I have tremendous respect for Dr. Katharine Hayhoe, an evangelical Christian and climate scientist at Texas Tech. Her walk and courage was an inspiration as I was cataloging the meteorological symptoms of a rapidly-changing climate. Professor David Titley is a friend, former classmate at Penn State, and a retired Navy Admiral. His ongoing focus on military implications of global climate volatility struck a chord. My old friend and mentor at WCCO-TV, Don Shelby, encouraged me to dig into renewable energy, focusing on solutions to this vexing challenge. Americans are already seeking out (clean) energy freedom, and a distinguished group of visionaries helped to frame the enormous opportunity, including Rolf Nordstrom at Great Plains Institute, Michael Noble at Fresh Energy, and Dr. Jonathan Koomey at Stanford University. Local climate science communicator Greg Laden and climate scientist Dr. John Abraham at the University of St. Thomas reviewed my manuscript, fact-checking and providing moral support along the way. I'm grateful for their patience and expertise.

I'm indebted to my agent, Dawn Frederick at Red Sofa Literary, for taking a chance on this project and representing me with style, grace, and humor. Editor Jeff Braun at Bethany House stepped up and took an interest in the message Mitch and I were sharing. So many days we feel like we're swimming upstream by encouraging a conservative approach to this unique challenge. But Jeff and his colleagues at Baker Publishing Group are demonstrating the courage of their convictions—that there must be a pragmatic, commonsense, small-government solution, one that leaves America more resilient and competitive; a market-friendly approach that jump-starts a sluggish economy. Less regulation, more Teslas.

My father taught me that conservatism and a respect for science are not mutually exclusive. Growing up, he reminded me that our family descended from eight generations of German *Forstmeisters* dating back to the 1600s. These were the experts who cared for Germany's forests. Maybe this love of nature is in my DNA, but I feel closest to God when I'm not only worshiping in a church but hiking in the woods—or fishing up at the lake—enjoying his awe-inspiring creation, a creation being threatened like never before.

Notes

Chapter 1: An Accumulation of "Coincidences"

1. "Odd-Ball Winter Weather," National Wildlife Federation, 2010, http://www. nwf.org/~/media/PDFs/Global-Warming/NWF_WinterWeather_Medium_REV. ashx.

2. CAIT Climate Data Explorer, World Resources Institute, http://cait.wri.org/ historical/Country%20GHG%20Emissions?indicator[]=Total%20CO2%20Emis sions%20Excluding%20Land-Use%20Change%20and%20Forestry&year[]=2012& focus=&chartType=geo.

3. Thom Patterson, "Will Hacking Nature Protect Us from Climate Change?" CNN, October 27, 2015, http://www.cnn.com/2015/10/26/tech/pioneers-carbon -sink-geoengineering-climate-hack/index.html?sr=twCNN102615pioneers-carbon -sink-geoengineering-climate-hack.

4. "Billion-Dollar Weather and Climate Disasters," National Centers for Environmental Information, https://www.ncdc.noaa.gov/billions/.

5. "Stafford Act Declarations 1953–2014: Trends, Analyses, and Implications for Congress," Congressional Research Service, July 14, 2015, https://www.fas.org /sgp/crs/homesec/R42702.pdf.

6. Ruth Liew, "Disaster Resilience Key to Managing Climate Change, Say Insurers," *Sydney Morning Herald*, October 4, 2015, http://www.smh.com.au /business/banking-and-finance/disaster-resilience-key-to-managing-climate-change- say-insurers-20151002-gk01k8.html#ixzz3njSj9AWS.

7. Seth Borenstein, "Go Figure: Figuring the Odds of Earth's Global Hot Streak," Phys.org, January 17, 2015, http://phys.org/news/2015-01-figure-figuring- odds-earth-global.html.

8. Helene Fouquet, "Want to See Climate Change? Come With Me to the Mont Blanc Glacier," Bloomberg, September 24, 2015, http://www.bloomberg.com/news /features/2015-09-25/climate-change-on-mont-blanc-the-vanishing-mer-de-glace.

9. Borenstein, "Go Figure: Figuring the Odds of Earth's Global Hot Streak."

10. "Climate Change Fuels Record Hot Summer's Latest Heat Waves," Climate Nexus, September 4, 2015, http://climatenexus.org/messaging-communication/current -events/climate-change-fuels-record-hot-summer%E2%80%99s-latest-heat-waves.

11. James Hansen, et al., "Perception of Climate Change," *Proceedings of the National Academy of Sciences* 109 (2012), http://www.pnas.org/content/109/37 /E2415.full.pdf.

12. Gerald Meehl, et al., "Relative Increase of Record High Maximum Temperatures Compared to Record Low Minimum Temperatures in the U.S.," *Geophysical Research Letters* 36 (2009), http://www.washingtonpost.com/wp-srv/nation /documents/geophysical-research-letters.pdf.

13. Ker Than, "Heat Waves 'Almost Certainly' Due to Global Warming?" *National Geographic*, August 6, 2012, http://news.nationalgeographic.com/news /2012/08/120803-global-warming-hansen-nasa-heat-waves-science/.

14. Robert Kopp, et al., "The Deadly Combination of Heat and Humidity," *New York Times*, June 6, 2015, http://www.nytimes.com/2015/06/07/opinion/sunday /the-deadly-combination-of-heat-and-humidity.html.

15. Ken Caldeira, "Stop Emissions!" *MIT Technology Review*, November 29, 2015, https://www.technologyreview.com/s/543916/stop-emissions/.

16. A. Park Williams, et al., "Contribution of Anthropogenic Warming to California Drought During 2012–2014," *Geophysical Research Letters*, August 28, 2015, http://onlinelibrary.wiley.com/doi/10.1002/2015GL064924/full.

17. "Western Wildfires and Climate Change" Infographic, Union of Concerned Scientists, 2013, http://www.ucsusa.org/global_warming/science_and_impacts /impacts/infographic-wildfires-climate-change.html#.VdelCZeLj9o.

18. Minnesota State Climatology Office, DNR-Eco Waters, September 2010.

19. David Liebl, "Climate Change, Rainfall and Wisconsin Communities," Wisconsin Initiative on Climate Change Impacts, July 2014, http://www.wicci .wisc.edu/uploads/ALNC%207-24-14.pdf.

20. Doyle Rice, "S.C. Flood Is 6th 1,000-Year Rain Since 2010," *USA Today*, October 5, 2015, http://www.usatoday.com/story/weather/2015/10/05/south-carolina -flooding-climate-change/73385778/.

21. Seth Westra, et al., "Global Increasing Trends in Annual Maximum Daily Precipitation," *Journal of Climate* (May 2013), http://journals.ametsoc.org/doi /abs/10.1175/JCLI-D-12-00502.1.

22. John Walsh and Donald Wuebbles, "Heavy Downpours Increasing," U.S. Global Change Research Program, http://nca2014.globalchange.gov/report /our-changing-climate/heavy-downpours-increasing.

23. "Essential Elements: Climate Change," American Academy of Actuaries, January 2015, http://www.actuary.org/files/EE_ClimateChange_012915.pdf.

24. Adam Voiland, "In a Warming World, Storms May Be Fewer but Stronger," reported in *Earth Observatory*, NASA, March 5, 2013, http://earthobservatory.nasa.gov/Features/ClimateStorms/page2.php.

25. "The Human Cost of Natural Disasters 2015: A Global Perspective," Centre for Research on the Epidemiology of Disasters, March 6, 2015, http://reliefweb.int/report/world/human-cost-natural-disasters-2015-global-perspective.

26. Justin Gillis, "Seas Are Rising at Fastest Rate in Last 28 Centuries," *New York Times*, February 22, 2016, http://www.nytimes.com/2016/02/23/science/sea-level-rise-global-warming-climate-change.html.

27. University of Illinois at Urbana–Champaign, *Cryosphere Today*, http://arctic.atmos.uiuc.edu/cryosphere/.

28. "The Facts About Sea Level Rise," Climate Central, http://sealevel.climate central.org/.

29. Climate Nexus, May 28, 2015. http://climatenexus.org/learn/planetary-systems/sea-level-rise.

30. Lewis Diuguid, "Climate Change Being Measured in Property Damage, Loss of Life and Costs in Billions of Dollars," *Kansas City Star*, April 16, 2015, http://www.kansascity.com/opinion/opn-columns-blogs/lewis-diuguid/article18690846.html.

31. Brandon Miller, "Expert: We're 'Locked in' to 3-Foot Sea Level Rise," CNN, http://www.cnn.com/2015/08/27/us/nasa-rising-sea-levels/.

32. Seth Borenstein and Dan Joling, "Warming's Recipe for Baked Alaska: Trillions of Tons of Glaciers Gone, Millions Acres Burned," *Associated Press*, August 30, 2015, http://www.usnews.com/news/science/news/articles/2015/08/30/global-warming-carving-changes-into-alaska-in-fire-and-ice.

33. "As Ice Age Ended, Greenhouse Gas Rise Was Lead Factor in Melting of Earth's Glaciers," Boston College press release, August 21, 2015, http://www.eurekalert.org/pub_releases/2015-08/bc-aia082015.php.

34. Thomas Knutson, et al., "Tropical Cyclones and Climate Change," *Nature Geoscience*, February 21, 2010, http://www.nature.com/ngeo/journal/v3/n3/abs/ngeo779.html.

35. "Below-Normal Atlantic Hurricane Season Ends; Active Eastern and Central Pacific Seasons Shatter Records," NOAA, December 1, 2015, http://www.noaanews.noaa.gov/stories2015/120115-below-normal-atlantic-hurricane-season-ends-active-eastern-and-central-pacific-seasons-shatter-records.html.

36. "Ocean Acidification," Smithsonian National Museum of Natural History, http://ocean.si.edu/ocean-acidification.

37. Jennifer Francis and Stephen Vavrus, "Evidence for a Wavier Jet Stream in Response to Rapid Arctic Warming," *Environmental Research Letters* 10 (January 6, 2015), http://iopscience.iop.org/1748-9326/10/1/014005/article.

38. Keith Harding and Peter Snyder, "Examining Future Changes in the Character of Central U.S. Warm-Season Precipitation Using Dynamical Downscaling," *Journal of Geophysical Research* (December 5, 2014), http://onlinelibrary.wiley.com/doi/10.1002/2014JD022575/full.

Chapter 2: It's Not About Polar Bears

1. John 15:12: "My command is this: Love each other as I have loved you."

2. Billy Graham, "Answers," October 22, 2008, http://billygraham.org/answer/ive-always-been-concerned-about-the-environment-and-my-concern-has-grown-in-recent-years-with-all-the-talk-about-global-warming-and-the-need-for-alternative-energy-sources-and-things-like-that-why/.

3. "The Dignity of Life," Focus on the Family video, https://www.youtube.com/watch?v=Y63Ksd8yHa4.

4. "Allowing Natural Death," National Association of Evangelicals resolution (2014), http://nae.net/611/.

5. American Academy of Pediatrics, et. al., "Letter to U.S. Environmental Protection Agency," August 4, 2011, http://www.usclimatenetwork.org/resource-database/letter-to-lisa-jackson-mercury-and-air-toxic-standards-american-lung-association-and-more-letter-8.4.11.

6. Quoted by Ben Geman, "Evangelical Group Holds Firm on 'Pro-Life' Link to EPA Rule," *The Hill*, February 10, 2010, http://thehill.com/policy/energy-environment/209831-evangelical-group-holds-firm-on-pro-life-link-to-epa-rule.

7. John 10:10: "The thief comes only to steal and kill and destroy; I have come that they may have life, and have it to the full."

8. Leonardo Trasande, et al., "Public Health and Economic Consequences of Methyl Mercury Toxicity to the Developing Brain," *Environmental Health Perspectives* 113 (May 2005), http://www.ncbi.nlm.nih.gov/pmc/articles/PMC1257552/.

9. Leonardo Trasande and Yinghua Liu, "Reducing the Staggering Costs of Environmental Disease in Children, Estimated at $76.6 Billion in 2008," *Health Affairs* 30 (2011), http://content.healthaffairs.org/content/30/5/863.full.pdf+html.

10. Shaina Stacy, et al., "Perinatal Outcomes and Unconventional Natural Gas Operations in Southwest Pennsylvania," *PLoS ONE* 10 (June 3, 2015), http://journals.plos.org/plosone/article?id=10.1371/journal.pone.0126425.

11. Lisa McKenzie, et al., "Birth Outcomes and Maternal Residential Proximity to Natural GasDevelopment in Rural Colorado," *Environmental Health Perspectives* 122 (2014), http://ehp.niehs.nih.gov/1306722/.

12. "State of the Air 2015," American Lung Association, http://www.stateoftheair.org/2015/key-findings/people-at-risk.html.

13. Barbara Bloom, et al., "Summary Health Statistics for U.S. Children: National Health Interview Survey, 2012," National Center for Health Statistics, http://www.cdc.gov/nchs/data/series/sr_10/sr10_258.pdf.

14. Kenneth Bock, *Healing the New Childhood Epidemics* (New York: Random House, 2007).

15. Philippe Grandjean, *Only One Chance* (New York: Oxford University Press, 2013), xiii.

16. Philip Rosenberg, et al., "Estrogen Receptor Status and the Future Burden of Invasive and In-Situ Breast Cancers in the United States" (presentation, American Association for Cancer Research, April 2015), http://mb.cision.com/Public/3069/9755232/81b414b4ec298479.pdf.

17. Chun Yang, et al., "Most Plastic Products Release Estrogenic Chemicals," *Environmental Health Perspectives* 119 (2011), http://www.ncbi.nlm.nih.gov/pmc/articles/PMC3222987/pdf/ehp.1003220.pdf.

18. Hueiwang Anna Jeng, "Exposure to Endocrine Disrupting Chemicals and Male Reproductive Health," *Frontiers in Public Health* 2 (2014), http://www.ncbi.nlm.nih.gov/pmc/articles/PMC4046332/.

19. Kristen Hayes-Yearick, "Our Dog Died After a Neighbor Sprayed Pesticides," *Safer Chemicals, Healthy Families*, http://saferchemicals.org/stories/kristen-hayes-yearick-mother-and-activist/.

20. Grandjean, *Only One Chance*, x.

21. Bruce Lanphear, et al., "Protecting Children from Environmental Toxins," *PLoS Medicine* 2(3), March 29, 2005, http://journals.plos.org/plosmedicine/article?id=10.1371/journal.pmed.0020061.

22. Natasha Murray, et al., "Epidemiology of Dengue: Past, Present and Future Prospects," *Clinical Epidemiology* 5 (2013), http://www.ncbi.nlm.nih.gov/pmc/articles/PMC3753061/.

23. John Brownstein, et al., "Effect of Climate Change on Lyme Disease Risk in North America," *EcoHealth* 2(1), March 2005, http://www.ncbi.nlm.nih.gov/pmc/articles/PMC2582486/.

24. Kiersten Kugeler, et al., "Geographic Distribution and Expansion of Human Lyme Disease, United States," *Emerging Infectious Diseases* 21 (August 2015), http://wwwnc.cdc.gov/eid/article/21/8/pdfs/14-1878.pdf.

25. John Kanthungo, "A Statement on the Reality of Climate Change in Malawi: Why the Church Should Act," Assemblies of God Relief and Development Services, November 20, 2013.

26. Albert Sasson, "Food Security for Africa: An Urgent Global Challenge," *Agriculture and Food Security* (2012), http://www.agricultureandfoodsecurity.com/content/1/1/2.

27. David Zucchino, "Coal Ash Contamination Upsets Residents Near North Carolina Plants," *Los Angeles Times*, May 4, 2015, http://www.latimes.com/nation/la-na-coal-ash-pollution-20150504-story.html.

28. Nancy Rabalais, et al., "Dynamics and Distribution of Natural and Human-Caused Hypoxia," *Biogeosciences* 7 (2010), http://biogeosciences.net/7/585/2010/bg-7-585-2010.pdf.

29. Michelle Leighton Schwartz and Jessica Notini, "Desertification and Migration: Mexico and the United States," U.S. Commission on Immigration Reform, Fall 1994, https://lbj.utexas.edu/uscir/respapers/dam-f94.pdf.

30. Cadie Thompson, "Elon Musk Says the Current Refugee Crisis Is Just a Glimpse of What's Coming If the World Ignores Climate Change," *Tech Insider*, September 24, 2015, http://www.techinsider.io/elon-musk-on-refugee-crisis-climate-change-2015-9.

31. "2014 Quadrennial Defense Review," United States Department of Defense, March 2014, http://archive.defense.gov/pubs/2014_Quadrennial_Defense_Review.pdf.

32. "National Security and the Accelerating Risks of Climate Change," CNA Military Advisory Board, May 2014, https://www.cna.org/cna_files/pdf/MAB_5-8-14.pdf.

33. Stephan Faris, "The Real Roots of Darfur," *The Atlantic*, April 2007, http://www.theatlantic.com/magazine/archive/2007/04/the-real-roots-of-darfur/305701/.

34. Marshall Burke, et al. "Warming Increases the Risk of Civil War in Africa," *Proceedings of the National Academy of Sciences* 106 (October 2009), http://www.pnas.org/content/106/49/20670.full.

35. Marshall Burke, et al., "Climate and Conflict," *National Bureau of Economic Research*, Working Paper No. 20598 (October 2014), http://www.nber.org/papers/w20598.

Chapter 3: A Healthy Dose of Skepticism

1. "Climate Change: Evidence and Causes," National Academy of Sciences, n.d., http://dels.nas.edu/resources/static-assets/exec-office-other/climate-change-full.pdf.

2. Katharine Hayhoe, "Climate Change—Faith and Fact," *Moyers and Company*, September 24, 2014, http://billmoyers.com/episode/climate-change-faith-and-fact/.

3. "How Do Scientists Know That Recent Climate Change Is Largely Caused by Human Activities?" The Royal Society, https://royalsociety.org/policy/projects/climate-evidence-causes/question-2/.

4. "How Do We Know That Recent CO2 Increases Are Due to Human Activities?" *RealClimate*, December 22, 2014, http://www.realclimate.org/index.php/archives/2004/12/how-do-we-know-that-recent-cosub2sub-increases-are-due-to-human-activities-updated/.

5. "The Human Fingerprint in Global Warming: What the Science Says," Skeptical Science, http://www.skepticalscience.com/its-not-us.htm.

6. "What Role Has the Sun Played in Climate Change in Recent Decades?" The Royal Society, https://royalsociety.org/policy/projects/climate-evidence-causes/question-4/.

7. Terrance Gerlach, U.S. Geological Society, quoted in "Volcanic CO2," June 19, 2011, https://tamino.wordpress.com/2011/06/19/volcanic-co2/.

8. "CO2 Is Already in the Atmosphere Naturally, So Why Are Emissions From Human Activity Significant?" The Royal Society, https://royalsociety.org/policy/projects/climate-evidence-causes/question-3/.

9. "Climate Is Always Changing. Why Is Climate Change of Concern Now?" The Royal Society, https://royalsociety.org/policy/projects/climate-evidence-causes/question-6/.

10. "How Does Climate Change Affect the Strength and Frequency of Floods, Droughts, Hurricanes, and Tornadoes?" The Royal Society, https://royalsociety.org/topics-policy/projects/climate-evidence-causes/question-13/.

11. "A Paleo Perspective on Abrupt Climate Change," National Climatic Data Center, http://www.ncdc.noaa.gov/paleo/abrupt/story2.html.

12. "If the World Is Warming, Why Are Some Winters and Summers Still Very Cold?" The Royal Society, https://royalsociety.org/policy/projects/climate-evidence-causes/question-11/.

13. "*Science* Publishes New NOAA Analysis: Data Show No Recent Slowdown in Global Warming," National Oceanic and Atmospheric Administration, June 4, 2015, http://www.noaanews.noaa.gov/stories2015/noaa-analysis-journal-science-no-slowdown-in-global-warming-in-recent-years.html.

Chapter 4: We Are . . . Easter People

1. Christopher Wright, *The Mission of God* (Nottingham, UK: InterVarsity Press, 2006), 403.

2. The Lausanne Movement, "The Cape Town Commitment," 2011, https://www.lausanne.org/content/ctc/ctcommitment.

3. Genesis 2:15

4. Francis Schaeffer, *Pollution and the Death of Man* (Wheaton, IL: Tyndale, 1970), 41.

5. Lesslie Newbigin, *The Open Secret: An Introduction to the Theology of Mission* (Grand Rapids, MI: Eerdmans, 1978, 1995).

6. The Revelation of Jesus Christ to John (21:1–4).

7. C. Austin Miles (1868–1946), 1912.

8. N. T. Wright, "The Easter Vocation, Acts 10:34–43; John 20:1–18," (sermon, Durham Cathedral, Easter Morning, 2006).

9. John 15:12

10. Gender, Climate Change and Health Public Health & Environment Department (PHE), Health Security & Environment Cluster (HSE), World Health Organization (WHO), Avenue Appia 20 — CH-1211 Geneva 27 — Switzerland.

11. Nick Watts, et al., "Health and Climate Change: Policy Responses to Protect Public Health," *The Lancet* 386 (June 23, 2015): 1861–1914.

12. Rick Warren, *The Purpose Driven Life* (Grand Rapids, MI: Zondervan), 2002.

13. Pope Francis, *Laudato Si': On Care for Our Common Home* (Vatican City: Libreria Vaticana, 2015), 7.

14. Psalm 89:11

15. Andrew Louth, ed., *Ancient Christian Commentary on Scripture*, vol. 1, *Genesis 1–11* (Downers Grove, IL: InterVarsity Press, 2001), 45.

16. James Jones, *Jesus and the Earth* (London: Society for Promoting Christian Knowledge, 2003), 4.

17. For examples, refer to Exodus 22:5; Exodus 23:10–12; Deuteronomy 5:12–14; Leviticus 25:1–12.

18. John Calvin, *Commentary on the Prophet Isaiah*, vol. 2 (Grand Rapids, MI: Christian Classics Ethereal Library), http://www.ccel.org.

19. Jim Ball, *Global Warming and the Risen Lord* (Washington, D.C.: Evangelical Environmental Network, 2010).

Chapter 5: A Place for Faith and Science

1. Stephanie Kirchgaessner, "Moral Case to Tackle Climate Change Overwhelming, Says Lord Stern," *The Guardian*, September 10, 2015, http://www.theguardian.com/environment/2015/sep/10/moral-case-to-tackle-climate-change-overwhelming-says-lord-stern.

2. John Abraham, Professor of Thermal Sciences at the University of St. Thomas (Minnesota), quoted from personal conversation with author.

3. Alison Benjamin, "Stern: Climate Change a 'Market Failure,'" *The Guardian*, November 29, 2007, http://www.theguardian.com/environment/2007/nov/29/climatechange.carbonemissions.

4. Jonathan Koomey, personal interview.

5. Ronald Reagan speech to the National Geographic Society (1984), http://www.reagan.utexas.edu/archives/speeches/1984/61984a.htm.

6. Charles Mann, "How to Talk About Climate Change So People Will Listen," *The Atlantic*, September 2014, http://www.theatlantic.com/magazine/archive/2014/09/how-to-talk-about-climate-change-so-people-will-listen/375067/.

7. Darryl Fears, "More Than 5 Million People Will Die From a Frightening Cause," *The Washington Post*, February 12, 2016, https://www.washingtonpost.com/news/energy-environment/wp/2016/02/12/more-than-5-million-people-will-die-from-a-frightening-cause-breathing/.

8. "Traffic Fatalities Fall in 2014, but Early Estimates Show 2015 Trending Higher," National Highway Traffic Safety Administration, November 24, 2015, http://www.nhtsa.gov/About+NHTSA/Press+Releases/2015/2014-traffic-deaths-drop-but-2015-trending-higher.

9. Damian Carrington, "Four Billion People Face Severe Water Scarcity, New Research Finds," *The Guardian*, February 12, 2016, http://www.theguardian.com/environment/2016/feb/12/four-billion-people-face-severe-water-scarcity-new-research-finds.

10. "2014 Quadrennial Defense Review," United States Department of Defense, March 4, 2014, http://archive.defense.gov/pubs/2014_Quadrennial_Defense_Review.pdf.

11. Quoted by Lynne Peoples, "Climate Change Threats to 'the Least of These' Compel Evangelical Christians to Act," *Huffington Post*, April 8, 2014, http://www.huffingtonpost.com/2014/04/05/climate-change-evangelicals-poverty-health_n_5088537.html.

12. Matt Redman, "The Otherness of God," *Christianity Today*, September 7, 2004, http://www.christianitytoday.com/ct/2004/septemberweb-only/theothernessofgod.html.

13. Genesis 1:27: "So God created mankind in his own image, in the image of God he created them; male and female he created them."

Chapter 6: "Fear Not, for I Am With You"

1. Saffron O'Neill and Sophie Nicholson-Cole, "Fear Won't Do It," *Science Communication* 30 (March 2009): 355–379.

2. Quoted by Stoyan Zaimov, "TIME's 100 Most Influential People: Evangelical Christian Scientist Featured for Climate Change Work," *Christian Post*, April 24, 2014, http://www.christianpost.com/news/times-100-most-influential-people-evangelical-christian-scientist-featured-for-climate-change-work-118544/.

3. Hoonyoung Park, et al., "Nonlinear Response of Vegetation Green-Up to Local Temperature Variations in Temperate and Boreal Forests in the Northern Hemisphere," *Remote Sensing of Environment* 165 (August 2015): 100–108.

4. Debbie Dooley, interviewed by Diane Toomey, "Why This Tea Party Leader Is Seeing Green on Solar Energy," *Yale Environment 360*, March 26, 2015, http://e360.yale.edu/feature/debbie_dooley_interview_why_this_tea_party_leader_is_seeing_green_on_solar_energy/2859/.

5. Quoted by Joby Warrick, "Utilities Wage Campaign Against Rooftop Solar," *The Washington Post*, March 7, 2015, https://www.washingtonpost.com/national/health-science/utilities-sensing-threat-put-squeeze-on-booming-solar-roof-industry/2015/03/07/2d916f88-c1c9-11e4-ad5c-3b8ce89f1b89_story.html.

6. Paul R. Epstein, et al., "Full Cost Accounting for the Life Cycle of Coal," *Annals of the New York Academy of Sciences* 1219 (2011): 73–98.

7. Quoted by David Gutman, "Coal Not Coming Back, Appalachian Power President Says," *Charleston Gazette-Mail*, October 27, 2015, http://www.wvgazettemail.com/apps/pbcs.dll/article?AID=/20151027/gz01/151029546/1419.

8. "Xcel Energy Proposes Nation-Leading Transition from Coal Energy to Renewables," Fresh Energy, October 2, 2015, http://fresh-energy.org/2015/10/xcel-energy-proposes-nation-leading-transition-from-coal-to-renewables/.

9. Michael Silverstein, "Will Cars Ever Replace the Family Horse?" *The Moderate Voice*, April 28, 2009, http://themoderatevoice.com/30233/will-cars-ever-replace-the-family-horse/.

10. "General Mills Announces New Commitment on Climate Change," August 30, 2015, https://generalmills.com/en/News/NewsReleases/Library/2015/August /Climate%20Commitment/f2d31e87-0ab9-42ea-a1af-b97d301e8ad8.

11. "Food and Beverage Company Statement on Climate Change," Ceres, October 1, 2015, http://www.ceres.org/files/global-food-and-beverage-leadership -statement-on-climate-change.

12. "Oil and Gas CEOs Jointly Declare Action on Climate Change," OGCI, October 16, 2015, http://www.oilandgasclimateinitiative.com/news/oil-and-gas-ceos -jointly-declare-action-on-climate-change/.

13. Ken Cohen, "ExxonMobil, Paris, and Carbon Policy," *ExxonMobil Perspectives*, May 5, 2015, http://www.exxonmobilperspectives.com/2015/05/06 /exxonmobil-paris-and-carbon-policy/.

14. News release, "ExxonMobil Says Climate Research Stories Inaccurate and Deliberately Misleading," October 21, 2015, http://news.exxonmobil.com/press -release/exxonmobil-says-climate-research-stories-inaccurate-and-deliberately-mis leading.

15. Excerpt from resolution, National Association of Evangelicals, "Caring for God's Creation: A Call to Action," 2015, http://nae.net/caring-for-gods-creation/.

16. "The University of Texas at Austin Energy Poll," conducted September 2015, http://www.utenergypoll.com/wp-content/uploads/2014/04/October-2015-UT -Energy-Poll-Final2.pdf.

17. "Risky Business: The Economic Risks of Climate Change in the United States," Risky Business Project, June 2014, http://riskybusiness.org/site/assets/uploads /2015/09/RiskyBusiness_Report_WEB_09_08_14.pdf.

18. Marshall Burke, et al., "Global Non-Linear Effect of Temperature on Economic Production," *Nature* 527 (2015): 235–239.

19. Matthew 6:34

20. Lee Iacocca, *Iacocca: An Autobiography* (New York: Bantam Books, 1984).

21. Jigar Shah and Raj Pannu, "Here's Why the Green Energy Movement Is Red, White and Blue," *Fortune*, August 19, 2015, http://fortune.com/2015/08/19 /green-energy-america/.

22. Drew Haerer and Lincoln Pratson, "Employment Trends in the U.S. Electricity Sector, 2008–2012," *Energy Policy*, March 20, 2015, http://www.eenews.net /assets/2015/04/08/document_cw_01.pdf.

23. Tesla Motors, https://www.teslamotors.com/gigafactory.

24. "About Us," Bloomberg New Energy Finance, http://about.bnef.com/pre sentations/bnef-summit-2013-keynote-presentation-michael-liebreich-bnef-chief -executive/.

25. Giles Parkinson, "Morgan Stanley: Tipping Point Nears for Going Off Grid," Renew Economy, March 25, 2014, http://reneweconomy.com.au/2014 /say-investors-wake-solar-pro-sumers-24413.

26. Christopher Martin, "Buffett Scores Cheapest Electricity Rate With Nevada Solar Farms," *Bloomberg*, July 7, 2015, http://www.bloomberg.com/news /articles/2015-07-07/buffett-scores-cheapest-electricity-rate-with-nevada-solar-farms.

27. Galen Barbose and Naïm Darghouth, "Tracking the Sun VIII: The Installed Price of Residential and Non-Residential Photovoltaic Systems in the United States," NREL, Lawrence Livermore Laboratory, August 2015, https://emp.lbl.gov /sites/all/files/lbnl-188238_1.pdf.

28. "60 Years of Energy Incentives," Management Information Services, October 2011, http://www.misi-net.com/publications/NEI-1011.pdf.

29. Jesse Jenkins, et al., "Beyond Boom and Bust: Putting Clean Tech on a Path to Subsidy Independence," Breakthrough Institute, April 2012, http://the breakthrough.org/blog/Beyond_Boom_and_Bust.pdf.

30. "World Energy Outlook 2014," International Energy Agency, November 2014, http://www.worldenergyoutlook.org/media/weowebsite/2014/WEO2014 _LondonNovember.pdf.

31. "2014 Outlook: Let the Second Gold Rush Begin," Deutsche Bank Markets Research, January 2014, https://www.deutschebank.nl/nl/docs/Solar_-_2014_Out look_Let_the_Second_Gold_Rush_Begin.pdf.

32. Ed Thomas, "Is the Sun Rising on an African Solar Revolution?" BBC News, February 18, 2015, http://www.bbc.com/news/world-africa-31503424.

33. Learn more at http://www.m-kopa.com/.

34. Anthony Hobley, "The Rural Poor Aren't Going to Wait for Centralized Clean Coal," *Business Green*, September 9, 2015, http://www.businessgreen.com /bg/opinion/2424944/rural-poor-aren-t-going-to-wait-for-centralised-clean-coal.

35. Antonio Castellano, et al., "Powering Africa," McKinsey and Company Report, February 2015, http://www.mckinsey.com/industries/electric-power-and-natural-gas /our-insights/powering-africa.

36. Robert Rohde and Richard Muller, "Air Pollution in China: Mapping of Concentrations and Sources," *PLoS ONE* 10(8), August 20, 2015, http://journals .plos.org/plosone/article?id=10.1371/journal.pone.0135749.

37. "Ministry of Environmental Protection and Land and Resources Soil Pollution Bulletin," People's Republic of China, April 17, 2014, English translation, http://www.mep.gov.cn/gkml/hbb/qt/201404/t20140417_270670.htm.

38. "Over 60% of Underground Water Substandard," *China Daily*, April 24, 2015, http://www.chinadaily.com.cn/china/2015-04/24/content_20529263.htm.

39. "China's Underground Water Quality Worsens: Report," *Xinhua English News*, April 22, 2014, http://news.xinhuanet.com/english/china/2014-04/22 /c_126421022.htm.

40. Travis Hoium, "How Renewable Energy Jobs Are Changing America," *The Motley Fool*, December 6, 2014, http://www.fool.com/investing/general/2014/12/06 /how-renewable-energy-jobs-are-changing-america.aspx

Chapter 7: Silver Buckshot

1. Jonathan Chait, "This is the Year Humans Finally Got Serious About Saving Themselves From Themselves," *New York*, September 7, 2015, http://nymag.com/daily/intelligencer/2015/09/sunniest-climate-change-story-ever-read.html.

2. Amanda Little, "Will Conservatives Finally Embrace Clean Energy?" *The New Yorker*, October 29, 2015, http://www.newyorker.com/tech/elements/will-conservatives-finally-embrace-clean-energy.

3. Fareed Zakaria, *Fareed Zakaria GPS*, CNN, aired February 28, 2016, http://transcripts.cnn.com/TRANSCRIPTS/1602/28/fzgps.01.html.

4. Quoted by Grace Wyler, "A War Over Solar Power Is Raging Within the GOP," *New Republic*, November 21, 2013, http://www.newrepublic.com/article/115582/solar-power-fight-raging-gop.

5. Liz Hartman, "Top 10 Things You Didn't Know About Wind Power," U.S. Wind and Water Power Technologies Office, August 10, 2015, http://energy.gov/articles/top-10-things-you-didnt-know-about-wind-power.

6. "2014 Wind Market Report," http://energy.gov/2014-wind-market-report.

7. Elon Musk, "All Our Patent Are [sic] Belong to You," Tesla Motors, June 12, 2014, http://www.teslamotors.com/blog/all-our-patent-are-belong-you.

8. "Small Nuclear Power Reactors," World Nuclear Association, June 2016, http://www.world-nuclear.org/information-library/nuclear-fuel-cycle/nuclear-power-reactors/small-nuclear-power-reactors.aspx.

9. Ari Daniel, "A New Kind of Nuclear Reactor?" WBUR-FM, April 8, 2015, http://www.wbur.org/hereandnow/2015/04/08/nuclear-reactor-molten-salt.

10. "Fast Neutron Reactors," World Nuclear Association, April 2016, http://www.world-nuclear.org/information-library/current-and-future-generation/fast-neutron-reactors.aspx.

11. Don Shelby, personal interview.

12. Michael Noble, Executive Director, Fresh Energy, St. Paul, Minnesota, personal interview.

13. Lindsay Wilson, "America's Carbon Cliff: Dissecting the Decline in US Carbon Emissions," Shrink That Footprint, March 2013, http://shrinkthatfootprint.com/wp-content/uploads/2013/03/Americas-Carbon-Cliff.pdf.

14. Rolf Nordstrom, Great Plains Institute (www.betterenergy.org), personal interview.

15. Quoted by Darryl Fears and Angela Fritz, "Freakish Weather From the North Pole to South America," *The Washington Post*, December 30, 2015, https://www.washingtonpost.com/national/health-science/freakish-weather-runs-from-top-of-the-world-to-the-bottom/2015/12/30/61203efa-af2c-11e5-b711-1998289ffcea_story.html.

16. Sophie Vorrath, "Fossil Fuels Subsidies Cost World $5.3 Trillion a Year — $10m a Minute," *RenewEconomy*, May 19, 2015, http://reneweconomy.com.au/2015/fossil-fuels-subsidies-cost-world-5-3-trillion-a-year-10m-a-minute-27983.

17. Rolf Nordstrom, personal interview.

18. Kerstin Schnatz and Ranty Islam, "Private Sector Key to Fighting Climate Change, Richard Branson Says," *Deutsche Welle*, May 11, 2003, http://www .dw.com/en/private-sector-key-to-fighting-climate-change-richard-branson-says/a -17205012.

19. Citizens' Climate Lobby, "Carbon Fee and Dividend Explained," https:// citizensclimatelobby.org/carbon-fee-and-dividend/.

20. Michael Noble, Fresh Energy (www.fresh-energy.org), personal interview.

21. Ibid.

22. Rolf Nordstrom, personal interview.

23. Pope Francis, *Laudato Si': On Care for Our Common Home*, May 24, 2015, http://w2.vatican.va/content/francesco/en/encyclicals/documents/papa -francesco_20150524_enciclica-laudato-si.html.

24. Jonathan Koomey, personal interview.

Chapter 8: We Can Do It—With God's Help

1. For more information on the York Plan, see James McClure's book, *In the Thick of the Fight* (York, PA: *York Daily Record*, 2005).

2. Paul Denholm and Robert Margolis, "Supply Curves for Rooftop Solar PV-Generated Electricity for the United States," National Renewable Energy Laboratory, November 2008, http://www.nrel.gov/docs/fy09osti/44073.pdf.

3. http://www.nvre.org/

4. For more information on The Joseph Pledge, visit www.josephpledge.com.

5. To learn more about Ground Works-Midwest, visit http://www.groundworks -midwest.com/.

6. Austin Mitchel, et al., "Measurements of Methane Emissions from Natural Gas Gathering Facilities and Processing Plants: Measurement Results," *Environmental Science and Technology* 49 (2015), http://pubs.acs.org/doi/pdf/10.1021 /es5052809.

7. "Public Letter on Clean Power Plan," Evangelical Environmental Network, https://creationcare.org/climate-realists-energy-optimists/public-letter-on -clean-power-plan/.

8. Taylor, "The Conservative Case for a Carbon Tax."

9. Bob Inglis and Arthur Laffer, "An Emissions Plan Conservatives Could Warm To," *New York Times*, December 27, 2008, http://www.nytimes.com/2008/12/28 /opinion/28inglis.html.

10. Eli Lehrer, "The Republican Base Would Welcome the Right Messages on Energy Policy," *National Review*, October 6, 2015, http://www.nationalreview .com/article/425113/energy-policy-polling-republicans.

11. Taylor, "The Conservative Case for a Carbon Tax."

12. Andrew Moylan, "How to Tax Carbon," *The American Conservative*, October 2, 2013, http://www.theamericanconservative.com/articles/how-to-tax -carbon/.

13. Bill Gates, quoted by Jeff Goodell, "Bill Gates: The Rolling Stone Interview," *Rolling Stone*, March 13, 2014, http://www.rollingstone.com/culture/news /bill-gates-the-rolling-stone-interview-20140313.

14. "A Business Plan for America's Energy Future," American Energy Innovation Council, April 2012, http://www.americanenergyinnovation.org/wp-content /uploads/2012/04/AEIC_The_Business_Plan_2010.pdf.

15. "Restoring American Energy Innovation Leadership," American Energy Innovation Council, February 2015, http://americanenergyinnovation.org/wp-content /uploads/2015/02/AEIC-Restoring-American-Energy-Innovation-Leadership-2015.pdf.

Mitch Hescox serves as President/CEO of the Evangelical Environmental Network (EEN), the largest evangelical group dedicated to the care of God's creation. Hescox, the son of a coal miner, speaks nationally, has published numerous articles, and also contributed to *Sacred Acts: How Churches Are Working Together to Protect Earth's Climate* by New Society Publishers. He has testified before Congress, spoken at the White House, and appeared on CNN, NPR, PRI, MSNBC, and numerous radio programs, both Christian and secular. He was named one of the ten Environmental Religious Saints in the Huffington Post and one of the top-ten faith leaders to watch in 2015 by Center for American Progress.

Hescox is also a member of the National Association of Evangelicals' Board of Directors, a group that represents over 40,000 U.S. congregations. Prior to joining EEN, Hescox pastored Grace United Methodist Church in Shrewsbury Township, Pennsylvania, for eighteen years, and before the call to ordained ministry served the coal and utility industry as Director of Fuel Systems for Allis Mineral Systems. He and his wife live in Pennsylvania. To learn more, visit www.creationcare.org.

Paul Douglas is a nationally respected meteorologist whose career has spanned more than thirty-five years in television and radio. His broadcast positions took him from the New York City area and Chicago to the Twin Cities, his current home. A successful entrepreneur, he has appeared on *Nightline*, *The CBS Evening News*, MSNBC, and CNN. He also speaks regularly to community groups and corporations about severe weather and climate trends and writes a daily column for the *Minneapolis-St. Paul Star Tribune* and the *St. Cloud (MN) Times*. In 2004, he wrote a book about extreme weather, *Restless Skies* (Sterling Publishing).

Douglas serves on the Climate Science Rapid Response Team, providing meteorological input with climate scientists to media and government representatives. He is also on the board of EEN, the Evangelical Environmental Network, focused on finding faith-based solutions to the most pressing environmental challenge of our time. Douglas and his wife live in Minnesota. To learn more, visit pauldouglasweather.com.